Yuriy

"Aggression, Toxicity, Violence, Abuse. What We're Together For?"

Series: "Formula of Love."

Part No. 14.

2023.

About the Book:

This is a comprehensive study of the topic of aggressive and violent behavior in couple relationships. You will understand the causes of aggression and its relationship to personality characteristics. You will learn to recognize toxic people and understand what forms of abusive behavior exist.

You'll find answers to questions such as:

- What are harassment and victim-blaming?

- How is psychological violence related to power?

- What are the forms of economic violence?

- Why does a culture of silence promote violence?

Distinguish manipulation and protect yourself from aggression!

Content

"About the 'Formula of Love' Book Series 5

From the Author 7

About the Book 18

Aggression... 20

    Causes of Aggressive Behavior...23

Aggressiveness:...30

    Aggressive Reactions: 33

Passive Aggression:..34

    Aggression and Personality..44

Toxicity...47

    Tall poppy syndrome 51

    Negativity..54

    Misanthropy..56

    The Dark Triad..58

Aggression and Violence 60

Violence 64

    Violence and gender..66

    Biopsychosocial Basis of Violence...69

    Violence and Developmental Level...73

    Typology of Violence..76

    Vocabulary of violence..79

    Cycle of Violence:...85

    Intimate Partner Violence..94

    Domestic violence..98

Abuse 102
Control 106
Physical Violence 116
Psychological Violence 119
Sexual Violence 135
Economic violence: 143
Consequences of domestic violence 145
    Why interest is lost 147
    What destroys relationships: 149
The Four Horsemen of the Apocalypse: 151
What we're together for? 152
What happy families have in common 155
Conclusion 159
A Note: 161
Copyright and Sources 164

"About the 'Formula of Love' Book Series

The "Formula of Love" series of books is for anyone who seeks a deep understanding of couple relationships - men and women, beginners and experts, ages 18 to 80. These books outline the general field of romantic relationships and comprehend the general principles of building harmonious relationships. Everyone will find new knowledge and insights here.

Series of books "Formula of Love" will help you solve problems in your relationship with your partner.

It is devoted to the analysis of various subtleties and difficulties that can arise in a couple. It is about issues of love, respect, trust, happiness, conflict resolution and many other nuances.

Most books on these topics answer the question, "How?". How to change a partner's mind, how to resolve conflicts, how to find happiness, how to build a trusting relationship, etc. Answers to these questions are important, but to understand the meanings embedded in them, you need to go deeper into the material and answer more complex questions.

The "Formula of Love" series of books basically answers the deeper question, "Why?".

Why am I not happy, why do we fight all the time, why does my partner violate boundaries, why doesn't he or she love me, etc. To find the true answers to these questions, we need to examine some of the scientific theories that explain human behavior. Understand how the biology of the body influences the psychology and ethics of an act. To understand unconscious reactions and conscious actions. Recognize what personality types there are. Identify the influence of upbringing, cultural stereotypes, and gender attitudes. The emphasis is on personal insight and experiences, but with paired communication in mind. After all, a couple or family is a mutually influential system. The mistakes of one partner are always reflected in the mirror of the soul of the second. And it is possible to correct mistakes only through personal development.

The influence of the level of development on the quality of relationships, is the discovery of these books.

The point is that each person, moving from one level to the next, experiences a personal crisis. His value system changes: the previous set of values is devalued or loses importance, and a new one has not yet been formed. At this point, a person becomes especially vulnerable to possible attacks from a partner. If the partner is not supportive during this period, he can easily destroy the relationship, while the supportive one is able to strengthen the union even stronger.

The book "Developmental Level. Partner Maturity" is the core of the whole concept.

It binds contradictory conclusions into a single semantic construction and explains why the same recommendations are beneficial for one couple and destructive for another. After studying the books of the series "Formula of Love", you will be able to determine for yourself what advice will allow your couple to build a trusting and warm relationship, and what will only harm.

In each book, you will find answers to various questions. One part will tell you about the reasons for the conflict of your partner, another will reveal the secrets of successful communication, the third will clearly show why people cannot change the model of their relationship. The whole series is written as a single, popular science work.

All books from the series "Formula of Love" are interrelated and complement each other.

For example, the book "Level of Development. Maturity of the partner" reveals the problem of maturity of the partner, and the book "Science of relationships: love, partnership, harmony in a couple" explains the impact of this maturity on the quality of relationships. The book "Aggression, Toxicity, Violence, Abuse. Why Are We Together?"

reveals various aspects of domestic violence, the roots of which are described in the books "Biology of Relationships: Why People Form Couples" and "Culture of Love: Norms, Power, Ethics." The human value structure discussed in "The Need for Love. The value of relationships" is reflected in his personality, which is presented in the book "Personality Harmony: Self-Esteem in Relationships", etc.

Thus, to collect a mosaic of disparate facts into a unified understanding of the issue of happy relationships, it is worthwhile to familiarize yourself with the entire series of books "Formula of Love". This will allow you not only to learn how to solve problems in relationships but will also improve the quality of your life.

You will be able to form correct expectations from your partner and learn to adequately evaluate him and your actions. Understand the principles by which you can build harmonious relationships in a couple. You will understand the concepts and meanings of love, happiness, meaning of life, etc. You will be able to enjoy life and share the joy of your existence with your partner.

"The Formula of Love" is a revolutionary popular science publication that presents a fresh look at the concept of love and partner relationships. This series of books will enable you to realize mistakes and improve your relationship with your partner."

From the Author

At first glance, the idea of a romantic relationship is simple and obvious - to meet the man or woman of your dreams and live happily ever after with him. However, looking around, we see that not everyone succeeds in this. People make repeated attempts to find happiness in a romantic relationship or marriage, but the statistics of failures are frightening. Does this mean that the idea of a long and happy life together is unrealizable? Is it possible to build an ideal relationship with a partner? How to choose the right one and create a harmonious and cheerful couple? In these questions we will deal with in the books of the series "Formula of Love".

We'll dive into the very depth of the complexities that arise in couples. But to understand the essence of these deep - mental and biochemical processes, it will be necessary to rise to the top of understanding society, the hierarchy of power, the rights of the state, and the responsibilities of the individual. To understand the attitudes and restrictions imposed by the outside world, which may conflict with the inner idea of a harmonious and happy relationship between two people in love.

We all feel like we're experts on the subject of relationships.

We observe them from the outside and participate in them throughout our lives. We know everything about it, understand it, and have our own, of course correct, opinion. We know what is better and what is worse, what is right and what is wrong. But is it so?

Why then does every second marriage now end in divorce? After all, all these people also thought they knew everything about relationships. Why then are there so many problems in relationships: misunderstandings, irritation, resentment, conflicts, unreasonable expectations?

Of course, everything can be blamed on the partner. He is the one who misunderstood everything, reacted in the wrong way, he has the wrong values, he is conflictual and problematic, and generally does everything out of spite, while I'm fine! But is it so?

Any conflict is 50% caused by the behavior of each partner!

Choosing a partner, we all thought that he is a prince or a princess from a fairy tale. With him everything will be beautiful, pleasant and magical. But after a while, the evaluation of the partner leads to disappointment. Maybe it was just a wrong choice of partner?

But it was you who chose him, that is, it was your mistake of choice! The partner remained who he was. How did it happen that you were wrong? And what exactly is your mistake: in the choice of his status and cultural level, temperament, mental development or character, form of relationships, gender distribution of responsibilities, or is it the result of your wrong self-concept? In other words, is it you personally who made the mistake, or is there something more here that depends on both partners?

Then the question arises: where was the mistake made and is it possible to eliminate it? How to avoid mistakes in future relationships and find the right partner? The one with whom your life will become a fairy tale, where you will feel loved and happy.

But as Heraclitus said: "Everything flows, everything changes". In this context, a new question arises: how to guarantee that today, tomorrow, and the day after tomorrow you will remain equally close and interesting to each other?

On the one hand, the answers to these questions seem obvious and common knowledge, but on the other hand, choosing the right solution from the abundance of available information becomes a challenge. After all, it is important to find a solution that will be perfect for you and your partner. It will take into account individual characteristics and help to create a sustainable system of relationships.

Resolving these issues is the focus of the 'Formula of Love' book series.

I'm sure you will find answers to these and other related questions in these books. But please do not be deceived! If you hope to read the books fluently or listen to them in the background, the result will be low, as with any other learning. There will be no result if you are too lazy to do the assignments and recommendations. There will be no result if you do not answer yourself sincerely, from the heart, if you will twist your soul, falsify facts and distort arguments. Only hardcore, only active participation and deep reflection on the knowledge presented.

A little about myself: I'm a Ph.D. in technical sciences, so my thinking is analytical, instrumental.

Instrumental thinking involves the ability to select the appropriate tools or methods for a particular situation, adapt them to the conditions of the task, and apply various strategies and tactics in the process. It is related to the ability to analyze a problem, determine the necessary steps and apply the appropriate tools or methods to achieve the goal at hand.

When forming the course, I searched for working algorithms and effective schemes in romantic and family relationships. Therefore, the structure of the course is based on models, principles and regularities, rather than on the retelling of millions of varieties of situations, difficulties, and problems that arise for people during the period of acquaintance and further life together. The books will present working schemes and algorithms of both psychological mechanisms and general - social, biological and philosophical concepts that directly or indirectly affect the harmony in a couple.

Of course, attached to this his considerable and quite traumatic experience. I went through a divorce myself, and it pushed me to look deeper into the essence of the issue of relations between a man and a woman. I will explain a little more here, as many people perceive such experience as the author's failure in this matter, but the real life experience we acquire only by living it personally.

I was married for almost 30 years, and then something broke... that's what I thought at the moment when my ex-spouse and I were picking ourselves out of the psycho-emotional wreckage of many years of living together and making the decision to divorce. This trauma pushed me to study the mechanisms of harmonious relationships more deeply and to understand what happened and how to act in order to prevent this from happening. **The result was incredible!** Had I had the knowledge that is outlined in these books, the outcome would have been different - both in the quality of our relationship and in the bottom line.

In starting this work, I wanted to outline the basic principles of a happy romantic relationship in an accessible and easy-to-understand way. It seemed to me that if I gathered the existing tools into a single work, the final result would be a rigid construction in the form of a Formula of love. However, deep immersion in the problems of romantic relationships, led my search in those areas that at first glance to the issues of love and happy relationships have nothing to do with love and happy relationships. For example, I was surprised to discover that heredity predetermines the quality of relationships by 50%, or that upbringing forms another 25%. Of course, these numbers are approximate, as all people have individual differences.

This presented me with a difficult choice related not only to the length of the book but also to the style of presentation. Initially, I had planned to create a small book written in an accessible language, with a list of rules that, when followed in a couple, would at least reduce conflict and ideally help partners achieve unity and harmony. However, the depth of understanding I have gained over the five years I have been working on the book has required more detail and precise wording.

As a result, the volume grew to an entire series of "Formula of Love" books:

1. "The biology of relationships: why people form couples."
2. "Emotions and reason: keys to understanding relationships."
3. "Psychology of relationships: traumas, defenses, behavioral styles."
4. "The need for love. The value of relationships."
5. "How to find happiness: looking through the window of the world picture".
6. "Level of development. Maturity of the partner".
7. "The logic of love: thinking in relationships".
8. "Harmony of personality: self-esteem in relationships".
9. "Culture of love: norms, power, ethics".
10. "Choosing the ideal partner. Masculinity and femininity".
11. "The science of relationships: love, partnership, harmony in a couple".
12. "Motives for marriage: sex, family, education, money".
13. "Communicating with your partner. Manipulation. Managing conflict."

14. "Aggression, Toxicity, Violence, Abuse. What We're Together For?"
  15. "The Formula of Love."

The main value of these books is that all of the most important material on romantic relationships is collected in one place. A wide range of practical models and tools for understanding yourself and your partner are offered.

As I began writing these books, I had an unsolvable dilemma - how to write unambiguous advice for different people. After all, it's no secret that people are developed differently. One and the same phrase or recommendation, a young person in 20 years will understand one way, and the same person in 40 years will understand in a different way.

The solution was found in the scientific concept of developmental stages of Freud, Piaget, Erikson, Kohlberg and the work that unites these theories - "Spiral Dynamics".

The book "Developmental Level. Partner Maturity" is the diamond of the whole "Formula of Love" series.

It explains the difficulties and conflicts that arise between people, not only in romantic relationships but also in professional and personal life. The book explains how developmental level affects communication, perception of self and others, and the ability to cope with conflict and stress. It provides a scientific explanation of the difference in how partners understand the same situation. It shows the differences in values and expectations that can arise between people at different stages of development. And the general level of development is detailed by specific developmental lines such as emotional maturity, cognitive development, ego development, social and ethical development.

Five key elements form the basis of the study:

- Biopsychosocial structure of personality
- Conscious and unconscious perception

- Gender differences and their links
- Cultural norms and stereotypes
- Level of personal development of each partner

Such a complex and multilevel refraction revealed deep connections between seemingly unrelated ideas. This allowed me to build a hierarchy of different layers of meaning, which shows how one event influences another.

Despite the abundance of theories used in the work, I tried to maintain a popular scientific style of presentation, so that the book would be understandable to young people on the one hand and interesting to experienced partners or experts in the field of couple relationships on the other. Therefore, one of my leading tasks was to describe the general field of romantic relationships: what it is, what types of relationships there are, how to create trust in a relationship, etc.

Realizing that people are ruled by animal instincts, or more precisely, biological motivational programs, I began my work by exploring these issues, revealing how the biology of the body invades human psychology, as this aspect is constantly manifested in couple relationships. In this way, issues of heredity, the influence of hormonal background and even biorhythms were uncovered, which I described in the book **"Relationship Biology: Why People Form Couples"**.

Next, it was necessary to understand how physiological reactions are transformed into thoughts and feelings. To deal with the differences between men and women, to understand how temperament affects relationships with a partner. Of course, this part would be incomplete without comprehending emotions. This stage of work is outlined in the book **"Emotions and reason: keys to understanding relationships"**.

However, happy relationships are not only determined by the biological component of a person. Therefore, it was necessary to move from the biologically predetermined part of the personality to the psychological part and deal with the key question: what is psychological health? What mental health disorders are and how to define them, for example, when you go on a first date with your partner. Or to understand how disorders manifest themselves in romantic relationships and what to do about it. The book **"Relationship Psychology: Traumas, Defenses, Behavioral Styles explores these issues"**.

Further, continuing to be on the border of biology and psychology, we can clearly see the watershed between unconscious motivational impulses and conscious behavior. On one side are needs and on the other are values, as revealed in the book **"The Need for Love. The Value of Relationships."**

This distinction will be maintained in the next book, **"How to Find Happiness: A Glimpse into the Window of the World"**, which deals with the issues of cognition of the world in general and relationships in particular. It also touches upon such topics as partner's competence, his ability to realize your feelings and thoughts, the general level of knowledge, destiny, quality of life and creative abilities of a person.

However, at this point I encountered an insurmountable obstacle related to people's different understandings of the same event. For example, one partner seeks sensual experiences and the other seeks professional fulfillment. The former's motivations are centered on the interpersonal relationship in the couple, and he suffers from his partner's seeming coldness, while the latter partner has a different focus of attention. He also suffers because he feels that his partner does not support him in his career ambitions. The solution to such contradictions is found in the developmental stage theories discussed in the book **"Developmental Level. Partner Maturity."**

However, even this book did not answer all the questions about the complexity of building a happy relationship, because people think differently. One person tends to be detail-oriented, while the other tends to be abstract. One partner draws conclusions from disparate facts using what's called inductive reasoning, while the other categorizes meanings based on deduction. To understand why this happens, we turn to Piaget's theory of cognitive development, described in the previous book, to examine thinking schemas and address the issue of maladaptive schemas most often formed in childhood. Drawing on cognitive-behavioral therapy, we will discuss many other issues related to negativism, reflection, and logic. In the final installment of The Logic of Love: thinking in relationships, we will look at cognitive distortions and other thinking errors that cause tension and miscommunication in couples.

In the next installment, we will overlay the biological component of a person's personality with his or her social adaptation and determine what personality types there are and why personality traits are possible and even necessary to change. We will learn how to identify authoritarian and infantile partners. We will dive into the basis of personality, dealing with the "self-concept" and the "Five-Factor Model of Personality" in the book **"Personality Harmony: Self-Esteem in Relationships"**.

However, all the above-mentioned knowledge did not give me an unambiguous answer to the question - how to build a harmonious relationship with a partner, because the topic of socialization was not touched upon earlier. The thing is that cultural attitudes, absorbed by a person during his life, are often not realized by him. At the same time, we build all our thinking based on social norms and stereotypes. This task put before me deeper philosophical questions about the nature of power and human rights, which are expressed in the immorality of a partner or, on the contrary, in his highly moral behavior. You will read the answers I found in the book **"Culture of Love: Norms, Power, Ethics"**.

The next layer that explained the basis of cultural stereotypes and the behavior of people in couples was the gender separation into men and women. In order to understand the basis of men's and women's behavior and the masculine and feminine qualities they display, it was necessary to look back in time to the evolutionary psychology described in the first book. The point is that when we look at the historical development of society, many points related to masculinity and femininity are contrasted. This gives insight into how gender divisions are constructed in society, but most importantly, the trend of pair bonding becomes apparent. I hope that the answers I have found will not only help you become more aware of your femininity or masculinity, but also help you shape your future more clearly. Also, in the book **"Choosing the Perfect Partner. Masculinity and Femininity"** we will look at the main motives and schemes for choosing a partner and get acquainted with decision-making methods and the concept of interpersonal compatibility.

It was only at this stage of my work that I achieved a holistic understanding of romantic relationships, delving into issues of love, attachment, interpersonal boundaries, and the typology of interpersonal relationships. It turned out that these issues are related to time and age. Time is viewed in terms of stages of relationship development, and age is viewed in terms of dialectical contradictions between partners, which reiterated the importance of a comparable level of development on both sides. For example, the question was answered: where the personal boundaries for healthy and co-dependent relationships are.

I hope that you, dear readers, will find the answers to these and other difficult life questions in the book **"Relationship Science: Love, Partnership, Harmony in Couples"**, where, in addition to the above, you will also learn about the theory of social exchange and balances in couple relationships.

In the next book, **"Motives for Marriage: sex, family, parenting, money,"** we will go back to our biological nature again, looking at the importance of sex for a harmonious relationship. It is in this part that the meaning of marriage and family comes in. We will look at the basic principles of building a happy family as a system of two equal partners. We will explore the major family crises, including infidelity and divorce. We will learn how the birth of a child affects the psychological atmosphere in a couple. We will dive into parenting issues, examining it in terms of its implications for the child's happy future life. We will also learn about the cost of a child's life from birth to adulthood and consider building different family budget models.

Solving problems that arise in a romantic or family relationship requires quality communication from both parties. In the book **"Communicating with your partner. Manipulation. Managing Conflict"**, I will offer suggestions to help you improve your couple's relationship. We will look at a number of theories describing the principles of harmonious communication with your partner, as well as dive into problematic aspects of couple relationships such as manipulation, quarrels, and conflict. We will explore various behavioral and conflict management strategies.

The most uncomfortable part about understanding couple relationships, dealing with aggression and violence, will be addressed in the book **"Aggression, Toxicity, Violence, Abuse. What We're Together For"**. You will learn how to distinguish between passive aggression and toxicity, learn how a person's developmental level is related to violence, become familiar with the cycle of violence, and more subtly differentiate between different types of domestic violence and understand the implications of abusive relationships for couples.

Only such a comprehensive and multifaceted treatment of couple relationship issues provides an overview of the complexity that people face when they enter into romantic relationships. In the final book in this series on various aspects of romantic and couple relationships, which I've called **"Formula of Love"**, I'll summarize the results, highlight the key factors, and remind you of the formula for happiness. We will once again cross the linguistic barrier of emotional maturity to enjoy an openwork construction of meanings and feelings, unconscious and conscious, needs and values, within the framework of a harmonious couple relationship.

These books are universal. Their goal is to find basic constructs that strengthen couple relationships, not to justify any gendered behavior. After all, a "formula" implies inviolable principles that are universal. That said, there are certain peculiarities in their interpretation on the female or male side. The challenge is to understand these principles and learn how to manage one's behavior.

In the series of books "Formula of Love" you can learn the basic principles, strategies, and methods for creating and maintaining healthy and harmonious relationships.

I want to emphasize right away, and will remind you regularly, that because of the uniqueness of each couple and each person, not all principles may be applicable. These books serve as a basis for introspection and reflection, but in the end, all solutions and approaches should be personalized and adapted to your specific situations and needs.

This is where I will end the author's description of the work, but I will note one more technical point. In order not to repeat myself, I decided to link to chapters or parts of the text that explain or supplement the idea expressed. The result is an emergent effect, thanks to which you will be able to extract additional meanings from the same text viewed in different contexts.

About the Book

In the book **"Aggression, Toxicity, Violence, and Abuse. What We're Together For"** the reader will learn about various aspects of aggressive behavior in familial and romantic relationships, including its causes of aggression, forms of manifestation, and relationship to personality characteristics. We will analyze the concept of toxicity in detail, where we will look at phenomena such as "Tall Poppy Syndrome," negativism, misanthropy, and the "dark triad."

The second part covers the topic of violence: its biopsychosocial foundations, relationship to developmental level, typology, and specificity. Special attention is paid to intimate partner violence and domestic violence, including such forms as physical, psychological, sexual, and economic violence.

The book analyzes the effects of domestic violence and the reasons why interest is lost in relationships. Relationship destructive factors such as the Four Horsemen of the Apocalypse, which are negative communication patterns that can undermine a couple's stability, are examined.

The book concludes with "What We're Together For" where readers will find answers to the question of what brings happy families together and how to overcome challenges.

You'll find answers to many other questions in the book:

- Why do people become aggressive and what are the sources of aggression?
- What factors contribute to aggressive behavior?
- Why do men and women display aggression differently?
- How are aggressiveness and love related?
- What is passive aggression and how does it manifest itself?
- What are the main triggers that activate passive aggression?
- How to deal with aggression?
- How is a person's developmental level related to the manifestation of aggression?
- What is toxicity and why is it important to avoid toxic relationships?
- How is aggression related to violence?
- What are the similarities and differences between aggressive men and women?
- What forms of violence do men and women exhibit?
- How is violence related to a person's level of development?
- What is the cycle of violence and how can you determine what phase a partner is in?
- What types of violence occur in intimate relationships?
- Is there a difference between domestic violence and abusive behavior?
- Why do partners exhibit controlling behavior?

- How is psychological abuse related to power and relationship form?
- What are harassment and victim-blaming?
- Why does a culture of silence contribute to violence?
- What are some forms of economic violence?
- What factors destroy relationships in couples?
- Why do people stay in destructive relationships?
- What is important in building a happy relationship?
- What talents do partners who have achieved harmony as a couple possess?

This book will be a source of valuable knowledge for anyone who wants to understand the complex issues of aggression, toxicity and violence in relationships and seeks to build harmonious and healthy relationships.

Aggression

Aggression could be considered in the first part, relational biology, to map the relevant animal component of human beings. Psychology and sociology, however, find their own arguments to explain aggression.

Aggression - is motivated destructive behavior that contradicts the norms of human coexistence, harms the objects of attack, brings physical, moral damage to people or causes them psychological discomfort.

Sources of aggression:

- **Biological approaches** conceptualize aggression as internal energy released by external stimuli[1].
- **Psychological approaches** conceptualize aggression as a destructive instinct, a reaction to frustration, and an affect triggered by a negative stimulus[2].

---

[1] Book 2: Emotions and reason: keys to understanding relationships. Temperament

- **Social approach** links aggression between congeners to access to resources and reproductive opportunities. One of its most common functions is to establish a dominance hierarchy[3].

All these factors can interact with each other and influence the manifestation of aggression in different contexts and situations[4].

Aggression is a form of behavior aimed at causing harm or damage to another being or object.

It is important to note that aggression is not always negative or destructive, and sometimes it can be the result of self-defense or self-assertion[5].

Aggression can be physical or psychological and can manifest itself in various forms such as physical violence, verbal abuse, threats, manipulation, or even passive aggression.

Aggression can arise from various reasons, including:

- Biological factors: Hormonal factors, genetic predispositions, or neural processes can influence aggressive behavior
- Psychological factors: Feelings of anger, frustration, fear, or repression can provoke aggression.
- Social factors: The social environment in which an individual resides can also influence aggression. For example, if someone struggles to cope with social pressure, they may become aggressive.

---

[2] Book 1: The biology of relationships: why people form couples. Stress Theory. Book 3: Relationship psychology: traumas, defenses, behavioral styles. Defense Mechanisms, Coping

[3] Book 9: Culture of love: norms, power, ethics. Tournament and couples culture

[4] Book 1: The biology of relationships: why people form couples. Biopsychosocial structure of personality

[5] . Book 3: Relationship psychology: traumas, defenses, behavioral styles. Assertiveness

- Environmental conditions: Stress, overload, or resource scarcity can trigger aggressive behavior.

These mechanisms are often related to emotions such as fear, frustration, anger, feelings of stress, dominance, or pleasure, which are rooted in culture, and personality structure[6].

Two types of aggression are distinguished, which are different from each other:

- Instrumental aggression, which is purposeful and conscious.
- Reactive aggression, which often leads to uncontrollable actions that are inappropriate or unwanted.

It's important to note that aggression is different from assertiveness, although these terms are often used interchangeably in everyday life, such as when talking about an "aggressive salesperson".

Aggressive behavior is an individual or collective social interaction that is hostile behavior with the intent to cause harm or damage..

Main forms of aggression:

- Physical aggression - aimed at inflicting physical harm on another person, such as hitting, kicking, attempting to strangle, etc.[7].
- Verbal aggression - manifested in the form of threats, insults, taunts, crude jokes, and other forms of humiliating and insulting another person verbally. For example, during a quarrel, one of the partners began to insult and disparage the other using rude and demeaning words[8].
- Passive aggression - manifested in the form of ignoring the other person, avoiding contact, refusing help, deliberately delaying or refusing to fulfill obligations[9].

---

[6] Culture, Attitudes, Five-Factor Model of Personality, Emotions, Manipulation
[7] Physical Violence
[8] Abuse, Toxicity, Manipulation
[9] Passive aggression, Psychological abuse

Each of these forms of aggression can lead to serious consequences for the victim, so it is important to learn how to recognize aggressive behavior and how to counteract it.

Causes of Aggressive Behavior

A person's aggressiveness is not related to his or her gender but depends on the cultural (social) environment. For example, in one tribe, men and women are equally aggressive, whereas in a neighboring tribe, men are more likely to be aggressive than women[10].

In all societies, aggressive behavior is condemned, and the aggressor is punished regardless of whether his aggressive actions have affected his interests. This norm is realized by people in very early childhood, from at least eight months of age. Children learn aggressive behavior in society[11].

For example, a child who observes a parent who physically expresses anger is likely to use the same behavior. A child who observes a parent dealing calmly with anger is more likely to do the same behavior[12].

Biological Factors:

Genetic factors, such as the length of the CAG chain in the androgen receptor gene, can influence men's levels of physical aggression, which may have an impact on their behavior in romantic relationships. However, other genes that increase dopamine and norepinephrine activity may also play a role in regulating behavior and emotions in relationships[13].

---

[10] Book 9: Culture of love: norms, power, ethics. Culture
[11] Book 9: Culture of love: norms, power, ethics. Culture, Parenting
[12] Book 7: The logic of love: thinking in relationships. Attitudes
[13] Book 1: The biology of relationships: why people form couples. Hormones, Genetics

The influence of genetics on behavior is not the only factor, and other factors such as environment, learning, and life experiences can also influence people's behavior in romantic relationships[14].

Aggression is one of the active-defensive variants of response to a stimulus, which is explained by the innate need for safety[15].

In turn, the centers of aggression - the amygdala and posterior hypothalamus - are responsible for aggression (the brain's "fight" command). An interesting fact is that cancerous tumors in the amygdala may be the cause of manic behavior[16].

The associative frontal lobe and the cingulate gyrus are also worth mentioning, because behavioral (motor) reactions are developed through them: the cortex triggers movements, selects the program ("hit" or "run"), and the gyrus compares real and expected results, triggers the generation of "fast" emotions. Aggressive people have high activity in the amygdala and low activity in the cingulate gyrus[17].

Fast reactivity is influenced by adrenaline and noradrenaline, which are secreted by the sympathetic nerves and the brain matter of the adrenal glands. Therefore, it can be argued that these two hormones increase aggression[18].

The adrenal cortex produces corticosteroids, some of which (cortisol) control the metabolism of glucose in the body, especially enhancing its formation from other substances (proteins, fats). This effect is most often observed under stress, hence cortisol indirectly affects the level of aggression[19].

---

[14] Book 8: Personality harmony: self-esteem in relationships. Self-Knowledge
[15] Book 8: Harmony of personality: self-esteem in relationships. Needs, Instincts
[16] Book 3: The Psychology of Relationships: Traumas, Defenses, Behavioral Styles. Brain, Mental Disorders
[17] Book 3: The Psychology of Relationships: Traumas, Defenses, Behavioral Styles. Appraisal, Assertiveness
[18] Book 2: Emotions and reason: keys to understanding relationships. Temperament

In addition, hormones such as dopamine and serotonin influence aggression. The first interacts with the substantia nigra and the nuclei of the ventral plexus of the brain, hence, if there is a lot of dopamine, the movements are sharper, its reaction and the activity of the center of positive emotions increases. Serotonin, on the other hand, affects the center of negative emotions: its excess reduces the activity of this center (in other words, serotonin acts as an antidepressant), and thus, just like dopamine, it reduces the level of aggression in sufficient quantities[20].

Evolutionary Explanation of Aggression:

Like many other behaviors, aggression can be studied in terms of how it can help humans survive and reproduce or, conversely, hinder them from doing so. This cost-benefit analysis can be viewed in the context of evolution[21].

According to the male-warrior hypothesis, intergroup aggression may represent an opportunity for males to gain access to partners, territory, resources, and increase their status. Therefore, conflicts may have created evolutionary pressures to develop psychological mechanisms in males to initiate intergroup aggression[22].

Men and Women:

Gender plays an important role in human aggression. There are many theories that attempt to explain the results that males and females of

---

[19] Book 1: The biology of relationships: why people form couples. Stress Theory
[20] Book 1: The biology of relationships: why people form couples. Biopsychosocial Basis of Violence, Hormones
[21] Book 11: The Science of Relationships: love, partnership, harmony in a couple. Social Exchange Theory
[22] Book 10: Choosing the ideal partner. Masculinity and femininity. Masculinity, Heredity

the same species may have different aggressive behaviors. One review concluded that male aggression tends to cause pain or physical injury, whereas female aggression tends to cause psychological or social harm[23].

- Men are more likely to display physical aggression related to dominance and establishment of status in the group, as well as defense of their territory and partners.
- Women tend to indirect forms of aggression, such as suppression, manipulation and social exclusivity.

This is a general observation; the specific forms and causes of aggression may vary by culture, developmental level, and other factors[24].

Among the sex differences found in adulthood was that females have a higher scale of indirect hostility and males have a higher scale of attack (anger).

Another difference found was that men have 20 times higher testosterone levels than women[25].

Based on the above differences, an explanation for domestic violence emerges where women show verbal aggression and men show physical aggression[26].

There are several similarities and differences in male and female aggression.

Similarities:

- Both forms of aggression can be physical, verbal or psychological.
- Both men and women may commit violence in the home, at work, in public places or in relationships.

---

[23] Book 1: The biology of relationships: why people form couples. Sexual dimorphism
[24] Book 6: Developmental level. Maturity of the partner. Developmental Level
[25] Book 1: The biology of relationships: why people form couples. Hormones
[26] Violence and Gender

- Both men and women may use aggression to achieve their goals, to control others, or to defend themselves.

Differences:

- Men tend to be physically aggressive, while women tend to engage in psychological forms of aggression such as manipulation, criticism, or isolation[27].
- Women tend to use violence in relationships to protect themselves or their children, whereas men tend to use aggression to manage or control their partners[28].
- Men tend to exhibit brutal and overt violence that can result in serious injury or even death, while women tend to exhibit subtle forms of violence that may be less visible but can also be harmful to the victim[29].

However, it should be noted that all of these differences and similarities are general trends, and there may be many individual differences and exceptions in each case.

Aggression in Relationships:

Research shows that romantic relationships in adolescence can reduce the level of aggression in both men and women, but women tend to decrease their aggression faster. This is influenced by social norms and standards of behavior[30].

For example, feminine women who conform to societal norms may appear more desirable to their partners, while aggressive women are often seen as antisocial and may struggle to fit into society[31].

---

[27] Manipulation, Physical Violence, Sexual Violence
[28] Book 1: The biology of relationships: why people form couples. Control, Sexual Dimorphism
[29] Book 2: Emotions and reason: keys to understanding relationships. Emotional Self-Regulation
[30] Violence and Gender

Despite female aggression not being considered the norm in society and potentially hindering the ability to find a partner, new statistical data shows an increasing number of women being arrested for domestic violence. However, this could be attributed to improved diagnostics and men becoming less hesitant to report violence from women, resulting in more female arrests, while the actual number of women perpetrating violence remains the same[32].

Aggression in men is correlated with social anxiety and stress.

The study indicates a positive correlation between social anxiety, stress and aggression in men. This means that when men have higher levels of stress and social anxiety, they are more likely to exhibit aggressive behavior.

Men with higher social skills have lower levels of aggression than those with lower levels of social skills[33].

In women, higher levels of aggression are associated with higher levels of stress, which in some cases of domestic violence, draws on the patriarchal breadwinner model[34].

Culture:

Aggression may manifest differently in collectivistic and individualistic cultures, and its manifestation may depend on the context of the romantic relationship[35].

- In a collectivist culture, where individual interests are usually subordinated to those of the collective, aggression may

---

[31] Book 10: Choosing the ideal partner. Masculinity and femininity. Femininity
[32] Social Constructivism, Sexual Violence
[33] Book 3: Relationship psychology: traumas, defenses, behavioral styles. Social Development, Assertiveness
[34] Book 11: The Science of Relationships: love, partnership, harmony in a couple. Patriarchy
[35] Culture, Gender

manifest itself in the form of pressure from others to conform to social norms and expectations.

For example, if two lovers do not follow the customs expected of couples in their culture, they may face criticism and even isolation from their collective. This can lead to conflict and aggression between partners, as well as feelings of depression and inexpressibility of their emotions

- In an individualistic culture, where individual interests are often placed above those of the collective, aggression can manifest itself in the form of competition between partners. For example, if two lovers place their personal successes and accomplishments above their relationship with each other, this can lead to conflict and aggression when they feel their personal goals are threatened because of their partner.

In both cultures, it is important to balance respect for the collective with individual rights and interests in order to create healthy and sustainable relationships. Open and honest dialog between partners can help resolve conflicts and reduce aggression in the context of romantic relationships[36].

Aggressiveness:

Although aggression has played a crucial role during human evolution, some psychologists argue that aggression is not inherently human. Children internalize patterns of aggressive behavior almost from birth[37].

Aggressiveness or hostility is a stable characteristic of a subject, reflecting his predisposition to behavior, the purpose of which is to cause harm to others, or a similar affective state (anger, rage, malice).

The causes of aggression can be various kinds of conflicts, including internal conflicts, while such psychological processes as empathy,

---

[36] Book 13: Communicating with your partner. Manipulation. Conflict Management. Communicating with your partner
[37] Book 12: Motives for Marriage: Sex, Family, Parenting, Money. Parenting

identification, and decentration restrain aggression, as they are the key to understanding others and realizing their independent value[38].

Decentration *is a characteristic of thinking, the ability of an individual to see different perspectives on an object.*

Since aggression requires significant energy and motivational expenditures, the term "aggressive" in relation, for example, to athletes, has come to be used as a characteristic meaning perseverance in overcoming obstacles and activity in achieving goals.

Aggressive behavior is aimed at the distribution and redistribution of resources.

Aggressiveness *is a manifestation of aggression or willingness to show it, its stimulant is the fear of resource scarcity.*

Resources can be food, reproductive values (partner, offspring), social status (power, income, prestige), territory, psychological comfort[39].

Aggressiveness and Love:

Eric Berne, stated that the force with which a person expresses his love and hate for others and for himself can be called aggressiveness. In Berne's context:

Aggressiveness *is the force that is used to express love, hate, pursue goals, and defend oneself.*

Berne emphasized that aggressiveness does not always have a negative meaning; it can be constructive and helpful in a person's life[40].

---

[38] Intrapersonal Conflicts, Social Norms, Violence and Level of Development, Thinking
[39] Book 11: The Science of Relationships: love, partnership, harmony in a couple. Patriarchy - Provider model
[40] Book 3: The Psychology of Relationships: Traumas, Defenses, Behavioral Styles. Mental Health

However, if aggression is expressed inappropriately or is harmful to others, it can become a problem and require correction[41].

Berne argued that understanding and recognizing one's aggressiveness and using it in accordance with social norms and values is an important part of personal development and establishing healthy interpersonal relationships[42].

People may hide their strong feelings by expressing them weakly, or they may display aggression with barely noticeable emotions[43].

Similar to the Rokeach's terminology, who distinguished between ends and means values, Berne also suggested that aggression should be viewed as an end and a means[44].

- Benign aggression (instrumental aggression) - describes forms of aggressive behavior that serve specific purposes and are not initially destructive. Such forms of aggression include pseudo-aggression and defense aggression. The latter form of behavior is usually complex in nature and often stems from a defensive response: "if you touch me, I will kill you".
- Malignant aggression (hostile aggression) is a maladaptive form of aggression that is unique to humans and has social rather than biological roots. It includes various forms of cruelty and violence, necrophilia, sadism and other manifestations. This form of aggression is the most pronounced and destructive, both for others and for the person himself[45].

Aggressiveness and violence:

---

[41] Toxicity, Family Therapy
[42] Book 11: The Science of Relationships: love, partnership, harmony in a couple. Relationships
[43] Passive Aggression
[44] Book 4: The need for love. The value of relationships. Values
[45] Violence

Aggressiveness and cruelty are often related to each other, but they are not the same concept.

Cruelty is a manifestation of harsh treatment and treatment of other living beings, which may be accompanied by pain and mental and bodily harm.

Cruelty means the deliberate infliction of suffering or pain on another being for no apparent reason or with an inducement to enjoy that suffering. Cruelty is usually associated with a lack of compassion, empathy, and moral awareness[46].

Aggressive behavior can become violent if its purpose is to intentionally cause suffering or painful feelings. However, not all aggression is violent, and aggressive behavior can be triggered by a number of factors, such as fear, defending territory, or self-defense[47].

Self-Aggression:

Aggressive actions directed at oneself are called self-aggression.

Self-aggression is an activity aimed at self-harm in physical and mental spheres.

Self-aggression (self-harm) can manifest itself in a variety of ways, such as:

- Physical self-harm, such as cutting or hitting oneself.
- Emotional self-harm, such as self-criticism, low self-esteem, or giving up one's own needs to satisfy a partner.
- Dependency on the partner, such as unwillingness to break up or to make decisions that do not take the partner into account.
- Self-isolation and avoidance of socializing with others.
- Sacrifice and willingness to suffer for the sake of the partner.

---

[46] Book 2: Emotions and reason: keys to understanding relationships. Emotional Intelligence, sections Culture, Developmental Level
[47] Book 1: The biology of relationships: why people form couples. Instincts, Needs

These behavioral patterns can be caused by a variety of factors, such as low self-esteem, problems with interpersonal relationships, depression, or anxiety.

If you notice these behaviors in yourself or your partner, it is important to talk about it and try to find ways to address the problem. You can see a therapist to help you understand the situation and learn healthy ways to communicate and behave in relationships.

Aggressive Reactions:

Types of aggressive reactions according to the Bass-Darkey questionnaire:

- Physical aggression - use of physical force against another person.
- Verbal aggression - expression of negative feelings both through form (shouting, screaming) and through the content of verbal responses (curses, threats).
- Indirect aggression - aggression directed at another person in a roundabout way or not directed at anyone, including sabotage, ignoring.

Sabotage - willful non-performance or negligent performance of certain duties, covert opposition to the implementation of something.

- Irritation - readiness to manifest negative feelings at the slightest excitement (temper, rudeness).
- Negativism - oppositional behavior from passive resistance to active struggle against established customs and laws.
- Resentment - envy and/or hatred of others for actual or fictitious actions.
- Suspiciousness - ranges from distrust and caution toward people to the belief that others are planning and doing harm.
- Guilt - expresses the subject's possible belief that he or she is a bad person, that he or she is doing bad things, and the remorse felt by the subject.

All types of these reactions, except for physical and overt verbal aggression, can be classified as passive aggression. Regarding verbal aggression, often disagreement or dissatisfaction is expressed in the hidden form of indirect aggression or manipulation[48].

Passive Aggression:

Passive aggression refers to a behavioral pattern in which aggression is expressed covertly and indirectly. Instead of overt confrontation or expressions of anger, people who exhibit passive aggression use the indirect ways of expressing their negativity described above[49].

Passive aggression - refusal of direct conflict, but disagreement is indirectly expressed.

This may include showing resentment, rebuking, ignoring, silence, suspicious behavior, sabotage, or passive resistance. Passive aggression can cause resentment or confusion in others because it implicitly interferes with constructive communication and problem solving[50].

Collectively, signs of passive aggression are noted by the term toxicity and manifest themselves in acts of psychological violence and controlling behavior[51].

Passive aggression correlates with cultural norms.

Cultural norms set the framework within which passive aggression is expressed. In one culture it may be a smile against a background of negative behavior, in another culture it may be a neutral facial expression against a background of sarcastic or hurtful words[52].

---

[48] Book 13: Communicating with your partner. Manipulation. Conflict Management. Manipulation
[49] Aggressive Reactions
[50] Book 3: The Psychology of Relationships: Traumas, Defenses, Behavioral Styles. Mental Health
[51] Toxicity, Psychological abuse, Controls
[52] Emotional Infection, Defense Mechanisms, Communication, Culture, Ethics

***Passive-aggressive behavior** is characterized by a pattern of passive hostility and avoidance of direct communication.*

Passive-aggressive behavior is characterized by avoidance of direct communication and manifestation of hostility through passive actions. These behaviors include ignoring expected social actions, such as being late for meetings or remaining silent in situations where a response is expected. Individuals who experience passive-aggressive behavior may experience anxiety because of the discrepancy between what they perceive and what the offending person displays.

Passive-aggressive behavior is described as a personality trait marked by a pervasive pattern of negative attitudes and characterized by passive, sometimes obstructive resistance to meeting expectations in interpersonal or professional situations. I note that the diagnosis of passive-aggressive personality has been removed from ICD11 because of frequent misapplication and the conflicting and unclear descriptions given by clinicians in the field. In ICD11, antisocial and narcissistic personality disorder has the greatest correspondence, but some manifestations are present in other disorders - depressive, paranoid, etc.[53].

Attribution of Hostility:

Passive-aggressive behavior is used as a name for a passive-aggressive style of behavior that is a frequent catalyst for conflict. Passive-aggressive behavior is based on incorrect interpretation (attribution) of other people's motives and behavior[54].

***Hostility Attribution** is a phenomenon in which a person attributes hostile intentions to other people (most likely unconsciously) in response to actions of these people that are essentially neutral.*

---

[53] Book 3: The Psychology of Relationships: Traumas, Defenses, Behavioral Styles. Personality Disorders
[54] Book 3: The Psychology of Relationships: Traumas, Defenses, Behavioral Styles. Behavior Styles, Interpersonal Conflicts, Assessment

A person who exhibits hostility attribution tends to see other people's behavior and interpret it as intentionally hostile or threatening. This phenomenon can be related to a variety of factors, including previous experiences, stereotypes, emotional state, and subjective beliefs[55].

Passive aggression is, of course, related to the biopsychosocial development of the individual and the different-level biopsychosocial programs described at the beginning of the aggression chapter[56].

Here are some examples of passive aggression in the family:

- Passive Neglect: A family member shows open indifference or ignores the needs or requests of other family members, does not answer their questions or does not pay attention to them.
- Silence and withdrawal: The family member refuses to communicate or maintain an emotional connection with other family members, shows coldness or avoids any conversation.
- Sabotage: A family member may intentionally do something that causes hardship or inconvenience to other family members, such as being deliberately late or forgetting family responsibilities.
- Passive resistance: A family member deliberately performs tasks incorrectly or carelessly, does not honor agreements, or refuses to cooperate with other family members.
- Denial and withdrawal: The family member adopts negative or negative attitudes toward other family members, fails to support them emotionally, and fails to show concern for them.

It is important to note that passive aggression may be less obvious and more difficult to identify than active aggression. It can cause significant damage to family relationships as it often leads to resentment, resentment and lack of communication[57].

---

[55] Book 4: The need for love. The value of relationships. Unconscious, Attitudes, Defense Mechanisms, Maladaptive Patterns, Stereotypes, Expectations of a Partner, Overton Window

[56] Biopsychosocial Structure of the Personality, Aggression, Violence and Developmental Level, Developmental Level section

Triggers of Aggression:

Aggression triggers are various situations, objects or actions that can cause aggressive behavior in an individual. They can be different for each individual because they depend on their personal experiences, perceptions and personality.

A trigger is a signal that automatically triggers some previously formed psychological and behavioral response.

Some common triggers for aggression:

- Frustration: when a person faces obstacles to achieving a goal, this can trigger aggression[58].
- Threat to self-esteem: when one feels that one's values, accomplishments, or self-esteem are being questioned, this can trigger an aggressive response[59].
- Resentment or injustice: feeling resentful or perceiving unfair treatment can trigger aggression[60].
- Painful or unpleasant stimuli: physical pain or unpleasant sensations can provoke aggressive behavior.
- Defense: if a person feels threatened by a threat to self or loved ones, this can trigger aggression as a defensive response[61].
- Competition: rivalry for resources, status, or power can trigger aggressive behavior[62].

---

[57] Book 2: Emotions and reason: keys to understanding relationships. Emotional contagion
[58] Defense Mechanisms, Expectations, Psychosexual Stages Theory
[59] Book 3: The Psychology of Relationships: Traumas, Defenses, Behavioral Styles.
[60] Book 9: Culture of love: norms, power, ethics. Justice Theory, Neuroeconomics
[61] Book 4: The need for love. The value of relationships. Needs
[62] Typology of Interpersonal Relationships

- Social learning: if a person grew up in an environment where aggression was considered normal behavior, he or she may react aggressively in certain situations[63].
- Chemical influences: use of alcohol, drugs, or certain medications can affect the brain and trigger aggression[64].
- Lack of sleep: chronic fatigue or lack of sleep can lower the threshold of patience and trigger aggressive behavior[65].
- Stress: constant tension and overwhelm can lead to aggressive reactions to stimuli[66].

Identifying aggression triggers in an individual can help them develop strategies for coping with aggression and improve their relationships with others[67].

Norm and Pathology:

Aggression is a social and emotional behavior characterized by the intent to harm another person or object. Aggression can be both normal and pathological, depending on the context, degree and causes of its manifestation.

Norm:

- Defense: Aggression can be normal and appropriate behavior when it is expressed in defense of oneself, loved ones, or one's territory from a real threat.

---

[63] Book 8: Harmony of personality: self-esteem in relationships. Identity
[64] Book 3: The Psychology of Relationships: Traumas, Defenses, Behavioral Styles. Mental Disorders
[65] Book 3: The Psychology of Relationships: Traumas, Defenses, Behavioral Styles. How relationship disorders manifest
[66] Stress Theory, Coping
[67] Book 3: The Psychology of Relationships: Traumas, Defenses, Behavioral Styles. Psychological Trauma

- Competition: In sporting and competitive situations, aggression may be acceptable when it is aimed at achieving success or overcoming an opponent within established rules.
- Setting Boundaries: In some cases, aggression may be displayed for self-assertion and to establish personal boundaries in a relationship. However, this type of aggression should be moderate and aimed at building a healthy relationship rather than harming the partner[68].
- Self-assertion: Moderate aggression can be useful in asserting oneself and setting personal boundaries, as long as it is done without harming others.

Pathology:

- Excessive aggression: Behavior is considered pathological when aggression is excessive, inappropriate, or uncontrolled. This can lead to relationship problems and social discomfort[69].
- Self-directed aggression: Aggression can also be pathological when it is directed at the self, which can manifest as self-destructive behavior such as self-harm or suicidal ideation[70].
- Baseless Aggression: Pathological aggression may manifest as baseless aggression toward others for no apparent or rational reason[71].
- Verbal Aggression: Negative communication, such as insults, humiliation, criticism, or rudeness, is a form of aggression that can cause emotional harm and undermine trust in relationships[72].
- Emotional Violence: Manipulation, control, dependency, and isolating a partner from friends and family are also forms of

---

[68] Book 3: The Psychology of Relationships: Traumas, Defenses, Behavioral Styles. Assertiveness, Boundaries
[69] Violence
[70] Aggression
[71] Mental Disorders, Mind, Biopsychosocial Personality Structure
[72] Toxicity, Psychological Abuse

aggression that can destroy relationships and cause emotional problems[73].
- Physical Violence: Physical aggression such as hitting, kicking, slapping, or other forms of physical force is a serious disorder and a highly unacceptable pathological form of aggression[74].
- Sexual violence: Coercion to engage in non-consensual sexual acts is also a form of aggression and violence[75].

Pathological aggression can have various causes, including genetic factors, upbringing, social environment, mental health disorders such as depression, anxiety disorders, or post-traumatic stress disorder (PTSD), as well as the influence of alcohol and drugs[76].

Aggressiveness in romantic relationships

Aggression in romantic relationships can come in many forms and can be negative for the health of the relationship. It is important to be able to recognize aggression and know how to deal with it[77].

Verbal aggression:

- a. Insults and humiliation
- b. Criticism and condemnation
- c. Yelling and rudeness
- d. Sarcasm and mockery

Emotional aggression:

- a. Manipulation and control
- b. Ignoring and coldness
- c. Threats of breaking up

---

[73] Emotional Contamination
[74] Physical Violence
[75] Sexual violence
[76] Book 1: The biology of relationships: why people form couples. Genetics, Heredity, Parenting, Mental Disorders
[77] Vocabulary of Violence

- d. Emotional blackmail

Passive-aggressive behavior:

- a. Not keeping promises and commitments
- b. Intentional lateness or neglecting the partner's needs
- c. Hidden criticism and holding grudges
- d. Avoiding responsibility and shifting blame onto the partner

Physical aggression:

- a. Pushing, hitting, and shoving
- b. Choking, strangling, and slapping
- c. Damaging the partner's personal belongings
- d. Threats of physical violence

Sexual aggression:

- a. Coercion for sex or unwanted touching
- b. Sexual assault or harassment
- c. Humiliating the partner in a sexual context
- d. Inappropriate comments or pressuring the partner

Financial aggression:

- a. Controlling the partner's finances
- b. Restricting access to money or threatening to withdraw financial support
- c. Demanding an account of the partner's expenses
- d. Financial blackmail or manipulation

Social aggression:

- a. Isolating the partner from friends and family
- b. Jealousy and controlling communication with other people
- c. Humiliating the partner in front of others
- d. Spreading rumors or false information about the partner

Healthy relationships are built on respect, trust, equality, and open communication.

How to deal with aggression?

The following steps should be taken to deal with aggression in romantic relationships:

- Define the problem: Recognize and define what exactly is aggression in your case[78].
- Communication: express your feelings and expectations about your partner's aggressive behavior[79].
- Set boundaries: identify what behaviors are unacceptable and communicate your boundaries to your partner[80].
- Work on yourself: if you are the aggressor, try to understand the reasons for your behavior and work on changing your reactions[81].
- Role reversal: try to put yourself in your partner's shoes to better understand their feelings and needs[82].
- Professional help: see a psychologist or therapist if aggression continues to disrupt your relationship and you can't handle the problem on your own.

If aggression becomes a persistent and pervasive problem, you may need to reevaluate your relationship and make decisions that are best for your well-being and happiness[83].

Here are some additional recommendations:

---

[78] Book 10: Choosing the ideal partner. Masculinity and femininity. Decision Theory

[79] Book 11: The Science of Relationships: love, partnership, harmony in a couple. Communicating with your partner

[80] Boundaries

[81] Book 2: Emotions and reason: keys to understanding relationships. Emotional Self-Regulation, Mental Health - Mental Self-Regulation, Coping, Behavior Styles

[82] Book 2: Emotions and reason: keys to understanding relationships. Emotional contagion

[83] Book 12: Motives for Marriage: Sex, Family, Parenting, Money. Family Crises

- Pay attention to red flags: if aggression occurs early in the relationship, pay attention to other red flags that may indicate a potentially toxic relationship[84].
- Create a safety plan: if you are in a dangerous or violent relationship, create a safety plan so you know what to do in case of an emergency. The plan should include contacts of friends, family, or organizations that can help you.
- Support: ask friends, family, or professionals for support. Talking about your experiences can help you cope with difficult feelings and situations.
- Learn strategies for coping with stress: aggression can be the result of not coping properly with stress. Learning techniques such as meditation, breathing exercises, or time-outs can help reduce aggression[85].

Remember that everyone deserves a safe, healthy, and loving relationship. If you are facing aggression in your romantic relationship, don't hesitate to ask for help and support. It is important to take care of yourself and your well-being so that you can build a happy and healthy relationship. The goal of a relationship is happiness and love[86].

Aggression and Personality

Some personality traits may influence the development of aggression:

- Tendency to act impulsively: People who are prone to impulsivity may exhibit more ill-considered and ill-considered aggression in response to stimuli or stressful situations.
- Emotional sensitivity: Individuals with higher emotional sensitivity may experience feelings of frustration, vulnerability, and discomfort more intensely. This may contribute to

---

[84] Boundaries, Toxicity
[85] Book 1: The biology of relationships: why people form couples. Coping Strategies, Mindfulness, The Biopsychosocial Basis of Violence
[86] Book 5: How to find happiness: looking through the window of the world picture. Happiness, Meaning of Life

aggressive reactions in response to emotionally challenging events.
- Thoughtfulness (instrumental aggression): People who have low thoughtfulness may exhibit more distracted and ill-considered aggressive behavior. They may not consider the consequences of their actions and tend to use aggression as a tool to achieve their goals.
- Hostile Attribution: People with hostile attribution tend to interpret any ambiguous situations or stimuli as hostile. They may see threats and hostility in other people's behavior even where none exists, which can contribute to aggressive reactions.

It is important to note that these personality traits may influence the development of aggression, but they are not the only factors. The development of aggression is due to the complex interaction of many factors, including environment, family upbringing, social factors, and individual life circumstances.

Five-Factor Model of Personality

Aggressiveness and hostility are personality characteristics that can be described using the facets of the Five-Factor Model of Personality:

- Impoliteness: expresses a lack of respect for others and manifests itself in the form of rudeness, offensive comments, and other forms of unpleasant behavior.
- Anger: reflects a tendency to feel anger and aggression in response to stressful situations and conflicts.
- Self-assertion: expresses the desire for self-expression and self-confidence in communication with others, can be manifested in the form of conviction in their rightness and manifestation of dominance.

- Power Struggle: reflects the desire for power and control in society, can manifest itself in the form of competition and pursuit of personal interests.
- Jealousy: expresses feelings of jealousy and envy of others, can manifest in the form of aggression and unkindness towards others.

These facets can reflect different aspects of aggressiveness and hostility in a person's behavior. However, it is worth remembering that each person is unique and can express his or her personality characteristics in different ways, so it is impossible to judge a person's behavior solely on the basis of the facets of the Big Five model, it is necessary to take into account all factors.

Aggression and Human Development

There are many factors that can influence a person's level of aggression and his or her overall development. Important factors include genetics, upbringing, experience with the environment, cultural norms and values, level of education and social skill development.

People who have more developed social skills and emotional intelligence tend to be less aggressive in their interactions with the environment. At the same time, people who have low levels of education or underdeveloped social skills may be more aggressive and violent.

Here are a number of studies that substantiate this claim:

- A 2002 study by Craig Anderson and colleagues found that aggressive behavior may be associated with low intelligence. Study participants with low intelligence showed more aggressive behavior compared to participants with high intelligence.

- A 2009 study by Alexander Todorov and colleagues found that people with high intelligence are less aggressive because they have better conflict resolution skills and know how to respond appropriately to situations that can trigger aggression.
- A 2016 study by Adrian Rayne and colleagues found that people with high intelligence may display aggression on occasion, but they do so more strategically and covertly. Thus, intelligence may influence the type and manner in which aggression is displayed.
- A 2018 study by Sarah DeFrias and colleagues examined the relationship between education level and aggression. The results showed that people with higher levels of education tended to be less aggressive, possibly because education improves communication and social interaction skills.

Overall, research findings indicate that a person's developmental level and intelligence can influence the manifestation of aggression.

A person's developmental level can influence his or her tendency to engage in aggressive behavior, but it is also important to consider the context and circumstances in which the behavior occurs. For example, the level of aggression can change depending on the situation and circumstances. For example, stress, depression, fatigue, or other factors can increase a person's aggressiveness.

Toxicity

In scientific psychology there is no term "toxicity"; this concept refers to everyday speech. Toxicity is used to describe people with whom communication evokes negative emotions[87].

Toxicity describes interactions in which participants' personal boundaries are blurred and the people themselves or their behavior are perceived as difficult, evoking hostile feelings[88].

---

[87] Book 2: Emotions and reason: keys to understanding relationships. Emotional contagion

When one speaks of toxicity in relationships, one is referring to the discomfort one feels when interacting with such people.

Toxic relationships *are relationships in which a person experiences negative feelings - anxiety, fatigue, insecurity, insecurity, and sometimes even fear.*

One of the main characteristics of toxic relationships is an imbalance of power and the shifting of responsibility and blame. Toxic people are adept at manipulation and provocation. They easily use reproaches, accusations, demands and claims. They are often skilled at lying, hypocrisy, and playing with the feelings of others[89].

Hypocrisy *is a moral quality that consists in attributing pseudo-moral meaning, lofty motives, and man-loving goals to knowingly immoral actions.*

It is virtually impossible to convince them of anything. Toxic people can turn into tyrants, seeking to control those around them. They are prone to catastrophizing, are jealous, envious, and like to impose their point of view[90].

Catastrophizing *is the exaggeration of dangers, threats, or bad outcomes.*

Often toxic people are characterized by acting skills and will do anything to maintain control of a relationship. They may portray changes in their behavior to make you think they have changed, but this is just another lie. You shouldn't expect your actions to bring about change in your relationship with a toxic person. People rarely change without a good reason[91].

Toxic people poison those around them with their negativism, lies and discontent.

Toxic people *are those who poison the environment and psyche of others, making their lives worse.*

---

[88] Book 3: The Psychology of Relationships: Traumas, Defenses, Behavioral Styles. Boundaries, Feelings
[89] Book 9: Culture of love: norms, power, ethics. Ethics
[90] Psychological Violence
[91] Cycle of Violence

You can find a lot of information on the Internet about how to recognize toxic people. Some of the traits that can give away a "toxic person" include a negative attitude, a tendency to judge, rudeness, lack of empathy, cynicism, anger, self-centeredness, exaggeration, and dramatization.

Exaggeration is the presentation of something as more extreme or dramatic than it actually is.

In general, the following signs of a toxic person are identified: - playing the victim, being resentful and unhappy with silence, seeing everything in a bad light, constant criticism and feeling jealous of others. Their judgment includes half-truths, sabotage, tardiness, failure to perform duties. They engage in gossip, lies, and misinformation. Manipulative practices are ubiquitous[92].

The victim game (self-victimization, victim card, or victim role fabrication), is a process in which a person falsifies or exaggerates their victim role for a variety of reasons.

Toxicity of one or both partners, destroys the relationship[93].

Toxic people show all the signs of passive aggression - irritation, negativism, suspicion, resentment, latent verbal aggression and guilt. Moreover, they label the guilt as something they supposedly experience, but in fact, through manipulation, the guilt is imposed on the partner[94].

Let me remind you of the types of passive-aggressive reactions:

- Indirect aggression - implicitly or covertly directed at another person.
- Irritation - readiness to manifest negative feelings at the slightest excitement (irascibility, rudeness).
- Negativism - oppositional behavior from passive resistance to active struggle against established customs and laws.

---

[92] Book 11: The Science of Relationships: love, partnership, harmony in a couple. Manipulation, Karpman Triangle
[93] Why Lose Interest, Divorce
[94] Aggression - Passive Aggression

- Resentment - envy and/or hatred of others for actual or imagined actions[95].
- Suspiciousness - ranging from distrust and caution toward people to the belief that others are planning and causing harm[96].
- Verbal aggression - expresses negative feelings through both the form (yelling, screaming) and the content of verbal responses (cursing, threats)[97].
- Guilt - expresses the subject's possible belief that he or she is a bad person, that he or she acts badly, and the remorse felt[98].
- Sabotage - inactivity, failure to fulfill obligations and requirements.

All of the above attributes are revealed in the position of the abuser or victim in domestic violence[99].

Let me remind you that the term "toxicity" has no clear scientific definition, and each person fills it with its own content. For one person, "toxicity" may be associated with crude jokes, for another with a lack of empathy, and for a third with physical violence. Because of this, it is difficult to recommend universal methods of defense. Still, there are some general strategies and approaches that can help people cope with toxic behavior in a variety of situations and relationships, as described in a number of previous chapters.

In order to cope with toxicity it is necessary to:

- Setting boundaries: Define your personal boundaries and respect them. Learn to say "no" and communicate openly about your expectations and limits. Do not allow others to violate your boundaries without you[100].

---

[95] Book 2: Emotions and reason: keys to understanding relationships. Misanthropy
[96] Paranoid Personality Disorder
[97] Antisocial Personality Disorder
[98] Psychological Violence
[99] Domestic Violence
[100] Book 11: The Science of Relationships: love, partnership, harmony in a couple. Boundaries

- Healthy Communication: Developing healthy communication skills will help you express your feelings, needs and expectations clearly and openly. Avoid aggressive or manipulative behavior and try to listen to others with an open mind and heart[101].
- Self-awareness and self-development: Work on improving your self-understanding by recognizing your strengths and weaknesses and developing strategies for coping with stress and frustrations. This can help you become more resilient to toxic behavior and learn to choose healthy relationships[102].
- Outside support: Seek support from friends, family, or professionals who can help you overcome toxic relationships and cope with negative emotions. Discuss your problems with people you trust and don't hesitate to ask for help[103].
- Developing empathy and understanding: Practicing empathy and understanding can help you better meet the needs of others and find common ground. Try to listen to others, put yourself in their shoes, and consider their feelings and needs[104].

And while the term "toxicity" can have different meanings for different people, these strategies can serve as a starting point for coping with toxic behavior and creating healthy, harmonious relationships[105].

One manifestation of toxicity can be "tall poppy syndrome".

Tall poppy syndrome

Toxicity can be a manifestation of perfectionism. A toxic perfectionist may express their expectations and high standards in such a way that

---

[101] Book 13: Communicating with your partner. Manipulation. Conflict Management. Communicating with your partner
[102] Book 1: The biology of relationships: why people form couples. Developmental Level, Coping
[103] Book 1: The biology of relationships: why people form couples. Developmental Level, Coping
[104] Book 2: Emotions and reason: keys to understanding relationships. Empathy
[105] Passive Aggression, Coping

they become unattainable or unrealistic for the other partner. They may criticize and condemn their partner for the slightest imperfections, constantly highlighting their failures and mistakes[106].

Perfectionism is the drive to achieve high standards, perfection and unadulterated success. People prone to perfectionism expect that they must be flawless and perfect, and they may also expect the same from their partners.

This creates an imbalance in the relationship, where one partner feels constant pressure and stress trying to meet the exorbitant demands of the toxic partner. Frustration and dissatisfaction on the part of the toxic partner can lead to feelings of inferiority and negative self-esteem in the other partner[107].

This can result in frequent conflict, emotional exhaustion, and even emotional or psychological abuse[108].

In these relationships, the toxic partner may use their perfectionist expectations as a means of controlling and manipulating the other partner. They may insist on correcting mistakes, humiliate and criticize their partner, and create an atmosphere of constant tension and unbalance[109].

The toxic partner, however, may be motivated by their feelings of inferiority or their inability to live up to such inflated standards[110].

Tall poppy syndrome is a term used to describe the social phenomenon of disliking and attacking people who stand out from the crowd because of their rare talents or outstanding success.

Tall poppy syndrome is similar to concepts such as envy, resentment, or jealousy of another's success. It manifests as a system of dominance and control where one partner, usually a man, acts as the leader and

---

[106] Perception Filters - Perfectionism
[107] Book 8: Harmony of personality: self-esteem in relationships. Self-Esteem, Milgram Experiment
[108] Abuse
[109] Control, Manipulation
[110] Mental Health

dictates rules and expectations to the other partner, usually a woman. However, the opposite can also happen if the woman has higher aggression[111].

The Tall Poppy Syndrome can create unrealistic expectations and limit the freedom and self-expression of the other partner. This can lead to dissatisfaction, inequality, and tension in the relationship[112].

The Tall poppy syndrome can be associated with patriarchal or unequal relationships. An example of high poppy syndrome is when one partner sets exorbitant standards for the other partner and expects him or her to meet those standards in all aspects of life. He or she may demand perfect appearance, impeccable behavior, constant support and attention, and no mistakes or conflicts[113].

The toxic partner, may demand that the other partner constantly reaffirm their love and commitment, sacrifice their interests and goals for the relationship, and avoid mistakes or faults. He or she may express excessive resentment and frustration if the partner does not live up to his or her ideals and expectations[114].

The tall poppy syndrome in patriarchal relationships is supported by stereotypes and norms inherent in a given culture or society, which affirm the role of the male as the authority and primary decision-maker in the family or society[115].

Often, toxic behavior reflects a partner's immaturity and inability to calculate the consequences of their behavior, which is consistent with the "crab mentality"[116].

---

[111] Passive Aggression, Leadership
[112] Book 11: The Science of Relationships: love, partnership, harmony in a couple. Typology of Interpersonal Relationships, Types of Relationships
[113] Interpersonal Conflicts, Harmony, Object Relations Theory
[114] Book 11: The Science of Relationships: love, partnership, harmony in a couple. Attitudes, Patriarchy
[115] Book 10: Choosing the ideal partner. Masculinity and femininity. Culture, Gender Stereotypes, Expectations
[116] Book 6: Developmental level. Maturity of the partner. Maturity

Crab mentality *is a concept that refers to a type of selfish behavior without considering long-term consequences.*

In the context of a romantic relationship, crab mentality describes a partner's selfish behavior without considering the long-term consequences of their actions for the good of the relationship and the partner[117].

A person with a crab mentality may be focused on his or her own wants, needs, and interests, ignoring or failing to consider the needs and feelings of the partner. Making decisions without consulting or agreeing with his partner, ignoring his partner's opinions and feelings, interpreting situations only from a position of self-interest. He may seek to maximize benefits for himself without considering the impact on his partner or the long-term well-being of the relationship[118].

Negativity
Negativism is one of the leading factors that destroys relationships.

---

[117] Book 1: The biology of relationships: why people form couples. Biopsychosocial Personality Structure
[118] Object Relations Theory, Leary Test

Negativism can manifest itself in constant criticism, skepticism, pessimism, complaining, and negative perceptions of the world around us. It is often accompanied by negative emotions[119].

Negativism is a psychological state or tendency in which a person tends to express and focus on negative aspects of life, situations, or relationships.

Negativism can be associated with a variety of factors:

- Psychological factors: Personality traits such as a tendency toward perfectionism, anxiety, low self-esteem, or a negative self-image can contribute to negativism. Also, some people may use negativism as a defense mechanism to lower expectations and avoid disappointment.
- Social Factors: The environment, including family, friends, or community, can influence the development of negativistic orientations. For example, if people around the individual often express negative views and criticism, this can influence and reinforce the individual's negativism.
- Experiential factors: Past negative experiences, traumas, losses, or failures can contribute to a negative orientation. Individuals may develop a negativistic perspective based on negative events and experiences from the past.

Negativism can have negative consequences for mental health and quality of life. It can interfere with positive interactions and relationships and make it difficult to find solutions and achieve goals[120].

Negativism in romantic relationships can manifest itself in a variety of ways:

- Constant criticism and negative attitudes: One partner may be constantly critical of the other, expressing negative attitudes

---

[119] Book 2: Emotions and reason: keys to understanding relationships. Emotional Intelligence, Evaluation, World Picture

[120] Book 5: How to find happiness: looking through the window of the world picture. Mental Health, Mindfulness

about his or her actions, statements, or appearance. This can create tension and unpleasant emotions in the relationship.
- Pessimistic view of the future: One partner may constantly express a pessimistic view of the future of the relationship, not believing in its success and expecting negative outcomes. This can create tension and stifle motivation for the couple's growth and development.
- Constant complaining and dissatisfaction: One partner may constantly express complaints and dissatisfaction about various aspects of the relationship, not finding the positives or joy in the partnership. This can affect the overall atmosphere and level of satisfaction in the relationship.
- Overcriticism and negative comparison: One partner may constantly compare their partner to others or to ideal standards, leading to a constant feeling of inadequacy and a negative perception of the partner.

Negativism in romantic relationships can create an unpleasant and tense atmosphere, hindering emotional connection and mutual understanding. It can intensify conflicts and lead to distancing of partners[121].

Misanthropy

Misanthropy is a negative, skeptical, or contemptuous attitude toward people in general or toward certain groups of people. Misanthropes often avoid society, preferring solitude, and may show distrust of others, believing people to be selfish, hypocritical, or hostile. Misanthropy may arise from negative life experiences, resentments, or disappointments in relationships with others[122].

Misanthropy *is a general hatred, dislike, distrust, or contempt for human kind, human behavior, or human nature.*

---

[121] Book 12: Motives for Marriage: Sex, Family, Parenting, Money. Family Crises
[122] Book 7: The logic of love: thinking in relationships. Negativism

It is worth noting that misanthropy is not always an enduring and unchanging worldview. Some people may experience misanthropic moods temporarily when faced with circumstances that cause frustration or distrust.

*A **misanthrope** or a misanthrope is someone who holds these attitudes or feelings.*

For those who want to overcome misanthropy, it is helpful to work on developing empathy, improving communication skills, and realizing that people are individuals with different motivations and values, and not all people follow negative stereotypes. In some cases, psychotherapy or cognitive-behavioral therapy can help to deal with misanthropy and improve relationships with others.

Negativism, misanthropy and toxicity

Negativism, misanthropy and toxicity are related and can influence each other, especially in the context of interpersonal relationships.

Consider the general relationship and implications of these terms:

- Negativism: A tendency toward a pessimistic view of the world can create resentment and mistrust of others. Negativism can contribute to misanthropy and toxicity in relationships, as one begins to see only the bad in others and expect the worst.
- Misanthropy: Negative attitudes toward people in general or toward certain groups of people can be the result of negativism. Misanthropy can exacerbate toxicity in relationships, as misanthropes often demonstrate distrust, avoidance of communication, and unwillingness to establish deep relationships with others.
- Toxicity: Toxic behavior in relationships can arise from negativism and misanthropy. Toxicity can manifest itself in various forms such as manipulation, emotional abuse, jealousy, and excessive jealousy. Toxicity can exacerbate

negativism and misanthropy, creating negative feedback loops and destroying relationships with others.

The implications of this relationship between negativism, misanthropy and toxicity:

- Decreased quality of life and overall well-being as the person may suffer from social isolation, stress and depression.
- Deterioration of relationships with others, including friends, family, and co-workers, due to negative attitudes and toxic behaviors.
- Development of self-fulfilling prophecies where negative expectations about other people and relationships are fulfilled due to toxic behavior and misanthropic beliefs, which in turn reinforces negativism.
- Loss of opportunities for personal and professional growth, as negative attitudes and toxicity can reduce motivation and ability to cooperate with others.
- Increased risk of developing mental disorders such as depression, anxiety, or personality disorders associated with negative outlook, misanthropy, and toxic relationships.

To break the negative links between negativism, misanthropy, and toxicity, it is important to be aware of one's thoughts, feelings, and behaviors, and to work on personal growth and the development of emotional intelligence. Helpful strategies include developing positive thinking, mindfulness, communication skills, empathy, and boundary setting. Which is essentially what self-development is all about[123].

The Dark Triad

In terms of psychology, the patterns of the dark triad of personality traits - narcissism, Machiavellianism, and psychopathy - that can be the basis of toxic behavior are distinguished.

The Dark Triad is a term in psychology used to describe three personality traits that are considered destructive and antisocial.

---

[123] Book 6: Developmental level. Maturity of the partner. Developmental level

The Dark Triad includes:

- Narcissism: Narcissistic individuals are characterized by excessive narcissism, a desire for power and superiority over others. They often expect those around them to admire and care for them. Narcissists can be disagreeable and insensitive to the needs and feelings of others[124].
- Machiavellianism: Machiavellians often manipulate others to achieve their goals without concern for the moral or ethical consequences of their actions. They can be cunning, cold, and calculating, using other people for their own gain[125].
- Psychopathy: Psychopaths are usually characterized by a lack of conscience, empathy, and guilt. They may be impulsive, aggressive, and unable to form emotional bonds with others. Psychopaths may also be characterized by a low degree of responsibility for their actions and their consequences[126].

Individuals with traits of the Dark Triad can pose serious challenges in social relationships and interpersonal interactions. They often display antisocial, manipulative, and aggressive behaviors, which can deteriorate the quality of life for those around them and lead to conflicts[127].

In general, any negative quality of a partner can be subsumed under toxicity.

And if we look at it objectively, most negative qualities will turn out to be constructive ways of adaptation, but manifested in excess or, on the contrary, too weakly. It can be a character trait or a situational strategy that the partner perceives inadequately[128].

---

[124] Book 8: Harmony of personality: self-esteem in relationships. Self-esteem
[125] Book 9: Culture of love: norms, power, ethics. Ethics
[126] Violence
[127] Book 3: The Psychology of Relationships: Traumas, Defenses, Behavioral Styles. Personality Disorders - Antisocial Personality Disorder
[128] Book 1: The biology of relationships: why people form couples. Biopsychosocial Structure of Personality, Coping, Perception Filters, Expectations from the Partner

Aggression and Violence

Aggression and violence are closely related but are different concepts. Aggression is behavior aimed at harming another person or object, while violence is the physical, psychological, sexual, economic or social infringement of another person.

Violence is the intentional use of physical force or power, actual or threatened, directed against oneself, another person, a group of persons, or a community that results in (or is highly likely to result in) bodily injury, death, psychological trauma, developmental disabilities, or harm of various kinds.

Aggression can come in many forms, including verbal aggression (insults, threats), social aggression (gossip, exclusion from the group) and physical aggression (hitting, shoving).

Not all forms of aggression necessarily lead to violence, but physical aggression can be one manifestation of violence[129].

Various factors can contribute to the link between aggression and violence:

- Individual characteristics: personality traits, upbringing, mental state, and biological factors can influence how a person displays aggression and violence.
- Social and cultural factors: social norms, societal expectations, and cultural traditions can influence the forms and extent of aggression and violence.
- Situational factors: stress, conflict, immediate threat or provocation can contribute to aggression and violence.
- Learning and perception: a person may learn aggressive behavior or violence through observation of others, from experience, or through the media.

Aggression can be a precursor to violence when individuals or groups begin to use aggressive behavior to achieve their goals or meet their needs. However, it is important to note that aggression does not

---

[129] Aggression

always lead to violence, and conversely, violence can occur without overt displays of aggression.

Violence without aggression and aggression without violence.

Violence without aggression and aggression without violence represent two different aspects of behavior and interaction.

Let us consider each of them separately:

- Violence without aggression: Arguably, violence without aggression can manifest as structural violence or unintentional harm. Structural violence occurs when social, political, or economic systems and structures result in discrimination, injustice, or infringement of human rights.
  For example, it may be systematic inequalities in access to education, health care or opportunities for social development. Such violence may be manifested without overt aggression on the part of certain individuals or groups.
- Non-violent aggression: Non-violent aggression usually manifests itself as verbal or psychological attacks that do not involve physical violence.
  Examples of such aggression include insults, threats, dismissive attitudes, sarcasm, cyberbullying, or other forms of manipulation and control. While such aggression does not cause physical harm, it can cause emotional distress, stress and anxiety, as well as negatively affect the victim's self-esteem and mental health.

Thus, violence can occur without aggression, but aggression is always expressed in some form of violence[130].

Aggression and violence.

---

[130] Typology of Violence

Aggression and violence can come in many forms and types that include physical, verbal, emotional, psychological, social and economic aspects.

Here are some of them:

- Physical aggression: It manifests itself through physical harm or threats against another person. This can include pushing, hitting, beating, and other forms of physical contact.
- Verbal aggression: Based on the use of words to insult, humiliate or provoke another person. This may include insults, swearing, threats, and crude language.
- Emotional Aggression: Involves using manipulation of another person's feelings in order to control, humiliate or harm. This can manifest itself through ignoring, manipulation, coldness and unwillingness to communicate.
- Mental Aggression: Includes the use of mental and emotional tactics to dominate, manipulate, or control another person. Examples include intimidation, isolation, fear, and threats.
- Social Aggression: Is based on the use of social networks and relationships to exclude, humiliate, or control another person. This can manifest itself through gossip, exclusion from the group, harassment and mobbing.
- Economic Aggression: Includes the use of economic means to control, manipulate, or harm another person. This can manifest through financial control, economic violence, threats of loss of employment or sources of income.
- Sexual Violence: This manifests itself through inappropriate sexual behavior, coercion or harassment that violates another person's rights and boundaries. This can include rape, sexual coercion, indecent touching and sexual harassment (harassment and pushing).
- Digital aggression (cyberbullying): This involves using media, the internet and mobile devices to insult, threaten, harass or humiliate others. Examples include posting offensive

comments or images, sending threatening emails or texts, and creating fake accounts to harass or blackmail.
- Direct aggression: Characterized by open and explicit expressions of aggressive behavior or intent, such as threats, physical violence, or insults.
- Indirect aggression: Characterized by covert and manipulative forms of aggression intended to cause harm without overtly expressing aggressive intentions. This can include gossiping, exclusion from social groups, and undermining another person's authority or reputation.
- Passive aggression: Expressed through unwillingness to perform duties, resisting, ignoring or remaining silent in response to requests or demands. It may manifest through avoiding responsibility, delaying tasks, or manipulating other people's feelings of guilt and frustration.
- Reactive aggression: A response to real or imagined provocative behavior on the part of another person. It is often perceived as a defense or counterattack in response to threat or hostility.
- Proactive aggression: Aimed at achieving specific goals or interests, and is often characterized by cold-blooded and deliberate aggressive behavior such as manipulation, control, or exploitation.

Each type of aggression correlates with certain forms of violence.

Violence

There is a strong correlation between levels of violence and modifiable factors in a country, such as concentrated (regional) poverty, income and gender inequality, harmful use of alcohol and lack of safe, stable and supportive relationships between children and parents[131].

Violence is the intentional use of physical force or power, actual or threatened, directed against oneself, another person, a group of

---

[131] Book 6: Developmental level. Maturity of the partner. Spiral Dynamics

persons or a community, that results in (or is likely to result in) bodily injury, death, psychological trauma, developmental disabilities or harm of any kind.

Interpersonal violence can be divided into two main categories:

- Domestic violence occurs between family members or loved ones, often in the home, including forms of violence such as child abuse, intimate partner violence (including marital rape) and elder abuse.
- Community violence occurs between people who may or may not be acquaintances and typically occurs outside the home. This category includes youth violence, random acts of violence, rape or sexual assault by strangers, and violence in institutions such as schools, workplaces, prisons, and nursing homes.

When interpersonal violence occurs in the family, its psychological effects can affect parents, children and their relationships in the short and long term.

Violence Across Generations

A common characteristic of abusers is that they witnessed abuse as children. Researchers who support this theory suggest that domestic violence may have three sources:

- Childhood socialization,
- Previous experience in relationships, and
- Levels of stress in a person's current life.

People who watch their parents abuse each other or are abusive themselves may incorporate violence into their behavior and into the relationships they establish when they grow up[132].

---

[132] Book 12: Motives for Marriage: Sex, Family, Parenting, Money. Parenting

Research shows that the more children are physically punished, the more likely they are to abuse family members, including intimate partners, when they become adults. People who were frequently beaten as children are more likely to endorse relationship violence, experience more family conflict, and experience more anger. Corporal punishment of children, such as whipping, spanking, or slapping, leads to weaker internal internalized values, low development of empathy, altruism, and resistance to temptation[133].

The Influence of Patriarchy

In some patriarchal societies around the world, a young bride moves into her husband's family. As a new member of the family, she starts from the lowest or one of the lowest positions in the family hierarchy and is often subjected to violence and abuse. She is also strictly controlled by her spouse's parents. When a bride comes into the family, the mother-in-law's status is elevated and she gains considerable power over someone else, often for the first time in their lives[134].

In many cultures, especially outside the West, social views of domestic violence vary considerably. In such societies, the relationship between husband and wife is seen as unequal, with an assumption of subordination of the wife to the husband. Some countries even enshrine this in their laws, for example, in Yemen, marriage laws require the wife to obey her husband and not leave the house without his permission[135].

Global studies of violence against women in the family and relationships show that in many countries, beating women is

---

[133] Book 5: How to find happiness: looking through the window of the world picture.
[134] Book 11: The Science of Relationships: love, partnership, harmony in a couple. Patriarchy, Culture of Silence, Binary Gender System
[135] Book 10: Choosing the ideal partner. Masculinity and femininity. Social constructivism

considered justified in some circumstances, especially in cases of perceived or actual infidelity on the part of the woman or her "disobedience" to her husband or partner. In such cases, violence against the wife is often not seen by society as a form of abuse, but is considered a reaction to the wife's behavior, for which she is seen as the perpetrator of the crime. In some places, even extreme forms of violence, such as honor killings, are endorsed by a significant part of society[136].

Violence and gender

Regarding the gender dimensions of aggression and violence, it can be said that although men are generally more aggressive, gender is not a reliable predictor of interpersonal aggression[137].

Research has shown that aggressive men and women, share a number of common traits:

- high levels of suspicion and jealousy;
- sudden and violent mood swings;
- poor self-control;
- higher than average approval rates for violence and aggression.

Men and women perpetrators of emotional and physical violence exhibit high levels of personality disorders. The frequency of personality disorders in the general population is approximately 15-20%, while approximately 80% of violent men in court-ordered treatment have personality disorders[138].

Moffitt et al. argue that men exhibit two distinct types of interpersonal aggression. One against strangers and the other against female intimate partners, whereas antisocial women rarely show aggression against anyone other than male intimate partners.

---

[136] Physical Violence, Psychological Violence - Victimblaming, Sexual Violence.
[137] Authoritarian Personality, Milgram Experiment, Gendered Brain
[138] Book 3: The Psychology of Relationships: Traumas, Defenses, Behavioral Styles. Mental Disorders

I note that in most countries women are forgiven violence against men, or rather men themselves do not report violence by women to the police. This is partly socially condemned, and partly a manifestation of gender stereotypes[139].

Female offenders have been found to have personality disorders associated with narcissistic and compulsive behavior. Unfortunately there are no objective statistics on female violence because social norms stigmatize female-on-male violence. The only available statistics are child abuse reports, which show that mothers physically discipline their children more often than fathers, while serious injury and sexual abuse are more often perpetrated by men[140].

In a 2007 study, Laurent et al. report that psychological aggression in young couples is associated with decreased satisfaction in both partners. This aggression can serve as a barrier to couple development as it blocks mature tactics. It is related to developmental level and inflated expectations of the partner[141].

Male and Female Violence

Male and female violence can manifest themselves in different forms and have different consequences.

Similarities and differences in male and female violence can be described in this way:

Similarities:

- Male and female violence can be physical, psychological and sexual forms of violence.

---

[139] Book 10: Choosing the ideal partner. Masculinity and femininity. Gender
[140] Book 3: The Psychology of Relationships: Traumas, Defenses, Behavioral Styles. Mental Disorders, Children
[141] Book 13: Communicating with your partner. Manipulation. Conflict Management. Expectations, Communication, Conflict)

- Both types of violence can be directed against loved ones or others, and can occur in the home or outside the home.
- Male and female violence can cause serious psychological and physical problems for the victim, including trauma, depression, post-traumatic stress disorder, and other psychological problems.

Differences:

- Male domestic violence tends to have more serious consequences for the victim than female violence.
- - Female violence may be more likely to manifest itself in the form of psychological abuse and controlling behavior, while male violence may be more likely to manifest itself in the form of physical violence[142].
- Male and female violence may have different motivations and causes. For example, male violence may be related to a desire to control a partner and establish one's power and privilege, while female violence may be related to self-defense or situations where a woman has no other options to protect herself or her children[143].

Overall, despite similarities and differences, both male and female violence present serious problems in society, and require immediate attention and action to prevent and reduce its impact on victims, and society as a whole.

Some studies show that the risk of violent behavior may be related to certain factors such as:

- Low or no education
- Low socioeconomic status
- Presence of problems in the family including violence between parents, unfavorable living conditions, etc.
- Mental health problems or drug and alcohol abuse

---

[142] Aggression
[143] Intimate Partner Violence

- Negative experiences with the justice system.

This does not mean that all people with the above factors will be prone to violence, but these factors may increase the risk of violent behavior. It is also important to realize that each case is different, and the causes of violence can be very diverse[144].

Biopsychosocial Basis of Violence

There are many biological, psychological, and social theories that look at the causes of violence in society.

For example, one biological theory states that violence may be related to genetic factors such as low levels of serotonin in the brain. Some studies suggest that people with low serotonin levels may be more prone to aggressive behavior and violence[145].

Psychological theories view violence as the result of childhood trauma. For example, physical or sexual abuse in childhood, lack of emotional support, or unfavorable environmental conditions. These factors can lead to mental health and behavioral problems that can be linked to violence[146].

There are also social theories that see violence as a result of inequality in society and social discrimination. They argue that violence can be caused by societal problems such as poverty, lack of access to education and health care, and lack of legal protection[147].

Developmental Level

I'll generalize these theories by the level of development, because according to the theory of double heredity, human behavior is formed

---

[144] Book 6: Developmental level. Maturity of the partner. Level of Couple Development - Games Couples Play

[145] Hormones, Aggression

[146] Book 12: Motives for Marriage: Sex, Family, Parenting, Money. Psychological Trauma, Parenting - Unhealthy Parenting Traits

[147] Book 5: How to find happiness: looking through the window of the world picture. Quality of Life, Human Rights, Milgram Experiment

on the basis of genetic and environmental factors. In other words, genetics sets the prerequisite, and environment shapes the final result[148].

Self-development, due to the neuroplasticity of the brain, can change the structure of personality. In this way, learning influences biology. A person can change his or her behavior on his or her own. This is supported by a body of research that shows that learning and experience can change brain structure and function[149].

For example, studies have shown that learning to meditate can change brain structure and function by increasing activity in areas related to attention control and emotional regulation. Social skills and empathy training can increase activity in brain regions associated with social perception and social skills[150].

This suggests that **self-development can change personality structure and behavior, including decreases in aggression and violence**. Teaching social skills, empathy, and effective conflict resolution can help reduce aggression and violence in society[151].

A number of studies have shown that:

- participants who received empathy training for 6 weeks showed decreased levels of aggression and improved social perception ability.
- training in effective conflict resolution can reduce levels of aggression.
- participants who received social skills training for 6 weeks showed decreased levels of aggression and improved social skills.

---

[148] Book 1: The biology of relationships: why people form couples. Heredity
[149] Book 2: Emotions and reason: keys to understanding relationships. Gender Brain
[150] Book 5: How to find happiness: looking through the window of the world picture. Awareness
[151] Book 1: The biology of relationships: why people form couples. Developmental Level, Emotional Self-Regulation

- inmate rehabilitation programs can reduce aggression and violence.

Program participants who received training and coaching for 6 months showed decreased levels of aggression and improved behavior.

This confirms people's ability to change their behavior, increase self-control, and reduce aggression and violent acts toward a partner[152].

Biopsychosocial Markers

In general, the causes of violence can be very diverse and can have various social, psychological and biological factors.

Here are markers that can be used to determine a partner's propensity for aggression and violence:

Biological Markers:

- High testosterone: This hormone is associated with higher levels of aggression and violence in some people.
- Low serotonin levels: Serotonin is a neurotransmitter that plays a role in regulating mood and behavior. Low levels of serotonin are associated with higher levels of aggression and violence.
- Low levels of monoamine oxidase A (MAO-A). This is an enzyme that breaks down mood-related neurotransmitters such as serotonin and dopamine. Low levels of MAO-A are associated with higher levels of aggression and violence.
- High cortisol: Cortisol is a hormone that is produced in response to stress. High cortisol levels are associated with higher levels of aggression and violence.
- High blood glucose levels: High glucose levels are associated with higher levels of aggression and violence.

---

[152] Book 8: Harmony of personality: self-esteem in relationships. Self-Concept

- Changes in brain structure: Changes in certain areas of the brain, such as the limbic system, are associated with higher levels of aggression and violence.

Psychological Markers:

- Low empathy: Empathy is the ability to feel and understand the emotions of others. Low levels of empathy are associated with higher levels of aggression and violence.
- Low self-regulation: Self-regulation is the ability to control one's emotions and behavior. Low self-regulation is associated with higher levels of aggression and violence.
- Low social skills: Social skills are the ability to interact with others and communicate effectively. Low social skills are associated with higher levels of aggression and violence.
- Low Emotional Intelligence: Emotional intelligence is the ability to recognize and manage one's own emotions and the emotions of others. Low levels of emotional intelligence are associated with higher levels of aggression and violence.
- Low empathy: Empathy is the ability to feel sympathy and compassion for others. Low levels of empathy and empathy are associated with higher levels of aggression and violence.
- Low decisiveness: Decisiveness is the ability to make decisions and act on one's beliefs. Low levels of decisiveness are associated with higher levels of aggression and violence[153].

Social Markers:

- Adverse parenting conditions: such as violence, substance abuse, parental divorce, are associated with higher levels of aggression and violence.
- Experiences of violence: when a person has been a victim of violence or witnessed violence, is associated with higher levels of aggression and violence.

---

[153] Book 10: Choosing the ideal partner. Masculinity and femininity. Decision Theory, Will

- Low socioeconomic status is associated with higher levels of aggression and violence.
- Negative attitudes towards society: such as cynicism, aggressiveness and misanthropy are associated with higher levels of aggression and violence.
- The desire for dominance and control is associated with higher levels of aggression and violence[154].
- Lack of social support: such as companionship, family and community support, is associated with higher levels of aggression and violence.

However, it is important to note that the presence of these markers does not necessarily mean that a person will exhibit aggressive behavior or violence, as many other factors, or their cumulative effect, can play a role in the development of violence and aggression.

Violence and Developmental Level

As you already realize, a person develops in different directions - emotional, cognitive, psychosocial, ego (development of the Self), moral, and others[155].

The relationship between developmental level and different types of domestic violence (physical, sexual, psychological, economic, and restraint) is complex and multifactorial[156].

I'll highlight some general trends that help explain this relationship:

- Emotional development: Lack of emotional maturity and self-regulation skills can make a person prone to impulsive actions, aggression and violence. This can manifest itself in all forms of domestic violence such as physical, sexual, psychological/emotional, and restraint[157].

---

[154] Five-Factor Model of Personality
[155] Book 1: The biology of relationships: why people form couples. Biopsychosocial Structure of Personality, Developmental Level, Self-concept
[156] Biopsychosocial Framework of Violence
[157] Book 2: Emotions and reason: keys to understanding relationships.

- Ego Development: A person with an unstable or inflated sense of self will be prone to dominance, control, and violence to reinforce their position and self-esteem. This may manifest itself in economic violence (e.g., controlling finances) and restricting the victim's freedom[158].
- Moral Development: A lack of moral values and a lack of understanding of justice, equality, and respect for others can contribute to the development of violent behavior. Low levels of moral development can manifest in all forms of domestic violence[159].
- Cognitive Development: Limited cognitive abilities or lack of education can make it difficult for an individual to develop skills in conflict resolution, empathy, and understanding other points of view. This can exacerbate the tendency toward violence in relationships[160].
- Social and Cultural Development: Social and cultural norms, stereotypes, and expectations also play a significant role in shaping violent behavior. In some cultures, or communities, abusive behavior may be normalized or even condoned, which contributes to its prevalence[161].
- Psychological factors: Mental health problems such as depression, anxiety, post-traumatic stress disorder (PTSD), or personality disorders can exacerbate violent tendencies. These factors can affect a person's ability to manage their emotions, interact with others, and make healthy decisions in relationships[162].

Emotional Intelligence, Emotional Development
[158] Book 3: The Psychology of Relationships: Traumas, Defenses, Behavioral Styles. Personality, Mental Health
[159] Book 6: Developmental level. Maturity of the partner. Ethics
[160] Book 7: The logic of love: thinking in relationships. Education, under Intelligence, Worldview, Thinking, Conflict
[161] Book 13: Communicating with your partner. Manipulation. Conflict Management. Culture, Communication
[162] Book 3: The Psychology of Relationships: Traumas, Defenses, Behavioral Styles. Mental Disorders, Toxicity

- Past experiences: People who have experienced violence themselves in their past (e.g., as children or in previous relationships) may be more prone to violence in their current relationships. They may reproduce patterns of violence they have encountered in the past, as this may be the only mode of interaction they are familiar with[163].

In each chapter of this book, I have pointed out the influence of developmental level on various aspects of human behavior, attempting to show the relationship between poor developmental errors and their consequences, which are summarized in this section, Violence.

Any form of violence is a consequence of prior mistakes, and mistakes indicate a low level of cognitive, emotional, or social development[164].

Relationship violence is a multifactorial phenomenon, and the causes can be varied, including social, cultural, economic, and psychological factors. Developmental level is only one component that can influence relationship violence.

Typology of Violence

A typology of violence is a systematization of different types of violence based on certain characteristics or criteria.

Based on the subjects of violence:

- Individual violence: committed by one person against another.
- Group violence: committed by a group of people against other groups or individuals.
- State violence: perpetrated or supported by state structures or agents of authority.

Based on the sphere of manifestation:

- Abuse: occurs within the family or domestic setting.

---

[163] Book 12: Motives for Marriage: Sex, Family, Parenting, Money. Parenting
[164] Book 6: Developmental level. Maturity of the partner. Developmental Level

- Labor violence: occurs within the employment relationship and in the workplace.
- Educational violence: occurs in educational institutions and in the educational process.
- Social violence: occurs in social and cultural spheres.

Based on the forms of manifestation:

- Physical violence: is the use of force or brute force against another person to cause physical injury or suffering. Example: Hitting, kicking, slapping, i.e., any type of physical contact that causes pain.
- Psychological abuse: is behavior intended to manipulate, control, or abuse another person, which may result in psychological suffering or harm. Example: Insults, humiliation, threats, and manipulation of feelings and destruction of self-esteem.
- Sexual violence: is any unwanted sexual act, attempted sexual act, harassment or comments made against another person's will. Example: Rape, sexual harassment, indecent propositions or touching.
- Economic Violence: is the use of financial resources and control over them to manipulate, limit the freedom or infringe upon another person. Example: Prohibiting work, controlling spending, forcing debts.
- Symbolic violence: Symbolic violence is the use of stereotypes, prejudice, and stigmatization to humiliate, degrade, or disadvantage another person. Example: Racist or sexist remarks, use of offensive symbols or images.
- Structural violence: is the systemic disadvantage of certain groups of people through social, political and economic structures and institutions. Example: Racial or gender discrimination, unequal access to education, health care, or opportunities for self-actualization.

Based on visibility:

- Overt violence: manifested in overt and visible ways, such as physical violence or insults[165].
- Covert violence: manifests in more subtle and less visible forms, such as manipulation, microaggressions, or structural violence.

Based on duration:

- One-time violence: incidents of violence that occur once or in isolation.
- Chronic violence: repeated violence that occurs systematically and over a long period of time[166].

Based on motives:

- Intentional violence: violence committed with the intent to cause harm, suffering, or disadvantage to another person.
- Unintentional violence: violence committed without a clear intent to harm, such as through negligence or unconscious bias.

Based on the impact on the victim:

- Direct violence: violence that directly affects the victim, such as physical violence or psychological pressure.
- Indirect violence: violence that affects the victim indirectly, such as through affecting people close to the victim or creating unfavorable living conditions.

Based on scale:

- Interpersonal violence: violence between individuals or small groups of people.
- Collective violence: violence between large groups of people or communities, such as ethnic conflicts or wars.

---

[165] Book 10: Choosing the ideal partner. Masculinity and femininity.
[166] Cycle of violence

Based on severity:

- Low severity (random acts of violence, rare occurrences)
- Medium severity (systematic violence but without serious consequences)
- High severity (systematic violence with serious consequences, up to and including fatal consequences)

Based on the nature of violence:

- Systematic violence (planned, deliberate, conscious)
- Incidental violence (unplanned, unplanned, occurring under the influence of emotion or stress)
- Reactive violence (violence in response to a partner's actions or behavior, may include self-defense)

Based on the dynamics of the relationship between partners:

- Unilateral violence (violence comes from only one partner)
- Reciprocal violence (both partners engage in violent acts against each other)
- Sequential violence (one partner carries out the violence and then the roles are reversed)

This typology is not exhaustive, and different types of violence may overlap and combine with each other in different situations. Nevertheless, it can be useful for analyzing and understanding the diverse manifestations of violence in society and for developing strategies to prevent and overcome it.

Vocabulary of violence

Just as in the conflict chapter, the vocabulary with which a person describes violence is extremely important. Perhaps it is in the violence part that specialized vocabulary is of maximum importance for a harmonious and happy relationship in a couple[167].

---

[167] Conflict vocabulary

Knowing this vocabulary for different forms of violence will help:

- Recognizing Violence: Identifying and understanding different forms of violence allows you to recognize potentially toxic situations, manipulations, and relationships. This helps you make informed choices about how to act and protect yourself.
- Preventing Violence: Knowing about these terms helps you identify and discuss relationship problems early on. This can prevent long-term damage to the relationship and improve the quality of interaction between partners.
- Help and Support: If you or someone you know is experiencing violence in a relationship, knowing about these forms of violence can help provide support, resources, and advice on what to do next.
- Education and awareness: Discussing these topics with friends, family or partners can help spread awareness about violence and its effects, which in turn can help create a safer and more understanding community.
- Personal growth: Becoming aware of different forms of violence can help you develop your own understanding of healthy relationships and set healthy boundaries with partners. It can also help you avoid repeating negative patterns of behavior in future relationships.

Particularly important are the first two points. If you can't distinguish between positive control and abusive behavior, or partner forgetfulness and gaslighting, it can lead a relationship to a pitiful ending[168].

In terms of overall structure, the following groups of violence can be distinguished:

- Forms of violence and aggression
- Manipulative methods
- Control and restriction of freedom

---

[168] Book 12: Motives for Marriage: Sex, Family, Parenting, Money. Divorce

- Negative relationships and dependencies
- Problems in communication and social interactions.

Let's take a closer look at the terminology, as knowing and understanding these terms will help you recognize and prevent potentially toxic situations and set healthy boundaries with your partners.

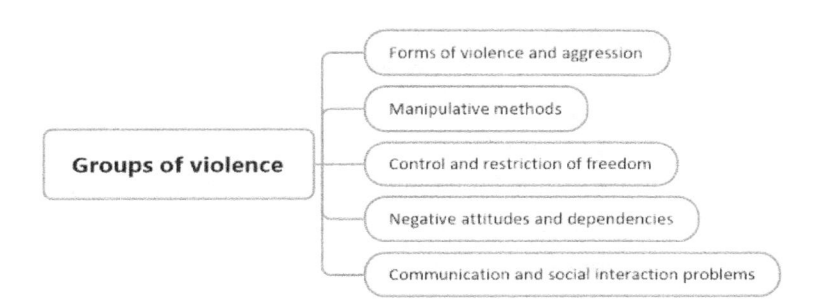

Groups of violence
- Forms of violence and aggression
- Manipulative methods
- Control and restriction of freedom
- Negative attitudes and dependencies
- Communication and social interaction problems

Forms of violence and aggression:

- Abuse - the use of power, control and coercion to subjugate another person.
  Example: a partner who controls finances and restricts access to the other partner's money.
- Physical violence - using physical force or the threat of physical violence to control another person.
  Example: assault, hitting, slapping, choking, grabbing.
- Sexual violence - using sexual force or the threat of sexual violence to control another person.
  Example: forced sex, sexual harassment, rape.
- Verbal violence - using insults, threats, and other forms of verbalization to control another person.
  Example: yelling, threats, cursing, taunting.
- Emotional violence - using destructive emotions such as fear, guilt, shame, and humiliation to control another person.
  Example: isolation, threats, humiliation, ignoring.

- Psychological abuse - using psychological tactics to control another person such as threats, control, manipulation, coercion.
  Example: gaslighting, projection, manipulation, ultimatums.
- Material and economic abuse - using control over finances or material resources to control another person.
  Example: financial control, restricting access to money, threats of loss of housing or other property.
- Intellectual violence - disregarding another person's opinion and refusing to recognize their rights to their opinion.
  Example: distrust of another's opinion, humiliation, denial of knowledge and expertise.
- Digital abuse - using electronic means to control, manipulate and manage another person.
  Example: cyberbullying, spying, controlling.

Manipulative Techniques:

- Gaslighting is a psychological technique used to confuse the victim and make them feel wrong and uncertain about their memories and experiences.
  Example: a partner who denies facts and reality to make the other partner doubt their memories.
- Triangulation - using a third person to cause jealousy and hatred in the victim and disrupt their relationships with others.
  Example: a partner who uses other people to cause jealousy in their partner.
- Projection (imposing one's feelings on another) - transferring one's own problems and shortcomings onto another person.
  Example: a partner who blames the other partner for something that is actually happening to themselves.
- Manipulation - using various tactics to control or change another person's behavior.

Example: a partner who uses threats, blackmail, and guilt manipulation to control another partner's behavior.
- Blackmail (moral or material) - using a threat to get the other person to do what you want.
Example: a partner who threatens to reveal a secret or do something unwanted to get the other partner to do what he or she wants.
- Ultimatums (demands to choose between options under pressure) - using a threat to make the other person choose between two unwanted options.
Example: a partner who demands that the other partner choose between a relationship with him or her and another important area of life.
- Lying and deception - using untrue statements or actions to make another person believe something that is not true.
Example: a partner who withholds information to get the other partner to do what they want.

Control and Restriction of Freedom:

- Neglect - lack of attention, care or concern for another person, which can lead to a lack of important needs and fulfillment.
Example: a partner who ignores or does not care about the other partner's feelings and needs.
- Control - an attempt to control the other person's behavior or their decisions.
Example: a partner who demands that the other partner do what they want rather than what the other partner wants.
- Isolation - restricting freedom of movement and contact with others. Isolation (physical, social or emotional) is often used to facilitate power and control over someone for the purpose of violence. Example: a partner who forbids the other partner from socializing with friends or family.

- Restraint - an attempt to control another person's behavior by limiting their freedom and decisions.
  Example: a partner who prohibits the other partner from doing certain behaviors, even if they are part of their personal life.
- Confusion (confusion, disorientation) - using tactics to confuse the other person and disrupt their understanding of the situation.
  Example: a partner who creates situations that may confuse the other partner and disrupt their decisions and behavior.

Negative Attitudes and Dependencies:

- Co-dependent relationship - an unbalanced dependence on another person that often leads to unhealthy relationships.
  Example: a partner who pauses his or her life to fulfill the needs of the other partner.
- Infidelity and cheating - breach of trust and marriage, cheating on one's partner.
- Jealousy and envy - an emotional state caused by the need to control and manage another person's relationships and behavior.
  Example: a partner who feels jealous of the other partner's interactions with someone else.
- Comparison with others - comparing and competing with others, which often leads to jealousy and insatiable relationships.
  Example: a partner who constantly compares the other partner to someone else and insists on changing their behavior.
- Approval Dependency (constantly seeking approval from a partner) - the need for approval and validation from another person, which can lead to unhealthy relationships.

Example: a partner who constantly seeks approval and validation from the other partner, even if it is detrimental to their own interests.

Problems in Communication and Social Interactions:

- Ignoring - ignoring the other person and their feelings.
  Example: a partner who ignores the other partner when they try to start a conversation.
- Ghosting (disappearing without explanation) - stopping communication and connection with another person without explanation.
- Mobbing or bullying (group bullying) - abusing and bullying another person in group situations. Example: a group of friends who systematically abuse and bully one of them.
- Stalking - unwanted harassment and violation of another person's privacy.
  Example: a partner who watches and observes another partner without their consent.
- Cyberbullying (virtual bullying) - violence and bullying through electronic means.
  Example: a partner who uses social media and messengers to humiliate and insult the other partner.
- Passive aggression - implicit and covert expression of aggression.
  Example: a partner who passively expresses their aggression through sarcasm and irony.
- Narcissism (excessive narcissism) - pathological self-love in which other people are seen as means to their own ends.
  Example: a partner who constantly talks about his or her own achievements and successes, ignoring the feelings and interests of the other partner.

These groups reflect different aspects of violence, manipulation and negative attitudes. A number of terms (victim-blaming, blame shifting, whistleblowing, etc.) will be further defined in the context of subsequent chapters.

Cycle of Violence:

Lenore Walker's theory, known as the "cycle of violence" or "cycle of violence theory", describes a recurring sequence of phases through which certain violent relationships pass.

***The cycle of abuse** is a pattern of behavior that can manifest itself in many forms of violence, including physical, psychological, sexual, and economic abuse.*

Walker originally suggested that the cycle of abuse described the controlling patriarchal behavior of men who felt entitled to abuse their wives in order to maintain control over them.

However, over time, studies of homosexual couples with the same cycle of abuse emerged, disproving the basis of male dominance over women[169].

Cycle of Abuse

1. Tensions Building
Tensions increase, breakdown of communication, victim becomes fearful and feels the need to placate the abuser

2. Incident
Verbal, emotional & physical abuse. Anger, blaming, arguing. Threats. Intimidation.

3. Reconciliation
Abuser apologizes, gives excuses, blames the victim, denies the abuse occured, or says that it wasn't as bad as the victim claims

4. Calm
Incident is "forgotten", no abuse is taking place. The "honeymoon" phase.

The cycle of violence consists of four phases:

---

[169] Book 11: The Science of Relationships: love, partnership, harmony in a couple. Typology of Interpersonal Relationships, Leary Test

1. Tension: The initial stage when conflict, tension and stress arise in a relationship. In this stage, there may be an accumulation of resentment, irritability, arguments and conflict.
2. Violent Episode: This is the active stage when violent acts occur. It may include physical, emotional, sexual, or economic abuse. The victim is subjected to aggression, threats, control, or other forms of violence.
3. Justification and Reconciliation Period: After an episode of violence, the rapist or abuser may resort to justifying their actions or attempt to reconcile with the victim. They may show remorse, apologize, or promise to change. The victim may be confused during this stage, having mixed feelings or hopes for positive change.
4. Lull: A temporary period when the violence temporarily stops, and the relationship may appear calm and safe. This may give the illusion that the cycle of violence has ended, but in fact it may happen again in the future.

The cycle of abuse can repeat itself many times over the course of a relationship. The duration and intensity of the phases can vary from couple to couple. It is important to note that not all violent relationships go through all phases. The presence or absence of a phase does not determine whether a relationship is violent or not[170].

Cycle of Conflict in Romantic Relationships or Marriage:

Tension phase. In this phase, there is a gradual build-up of tension between the partners. One of the partners may begin to exhibit aggressive or controlling behavior. The victim, in turn, may feel fear and try to appease the attacker to avoid conflict[171].

The couple's behaviors arise in the couple:

---

[170] Vocabulary of violence
[171] Book 13: Communicating with your partner. Manipulation. Conflict Management. Conflict Management

- Frequent arguments and disagreements: Constant arguments over small or significant issues, disagreements in opinions and desires can create a buildup of tension.
- Violation of boundaries and personal privacy: Failure to respect boundaries, invasion of personal space, or violation of privacy can cause tension and feelings of violation of personal intima.
- Financial problems: Disputes and disagreements over financial issues, such as allocation of money or misuse of financial resources, can be a source of tension.
- - Lack of support and emotional strain: Lack of emotional support, misunderstandings and inadequacy to meet emotional needs can lead to tension and conflict.
- - Control and jealousy: A partner may be overly jealous, demanding constant control or monitoring of the other partner's actions. This can create tension and a sense of restricted freedom. Which eventually leads to social isolation.

In the tension phase, partners may try to alleviate tension, but often without success. Direct violence may not yet occur, but tension and conflict may increase, setting the stage for the subsequent active violence phase of the cycle.

Violence outbreak phase. In this phase, an act of violence occurs, which may be physical, psychological, or sexual. Tension reaches its tipping point, and the aggressor commits violent acts against the partner. The victim may experience fear, pain and humiliation[172].

Here are some examples of how violence can manifest in this phase:

- Physical Violence: This includes direct physical violence such as hitting, pushing, choking, causing bodily harm[173].

---

[172] Book 1: The biology of relationships: why people form couples. Biopsychosocial basis of violence, Aggression and violence
[173] Physical Violence

- Emotional and psychological violence: This includes threats, insults, humiliation, manipulation, and other forms of violence that cause emotional and psychological pain[174].
- Sexual violence: This includes coercion or violent acts against a partner's sexuality, including forced sex, rape or other forms of sexual violence[175].
- Economic Violence: This includes controlling or restricting access to financial resource[176].

In the second phase of the cycle of violence, the violent episode manifests itself and may cause physical and emotional pain to the victim. The victim may experience fear, helplessness, low self-esteem, and psychological trauma. An episode of violence can have varying degrees of severity and duration. It can be one-time, recurrent or periodic, depending on the dynamics of the relationship and the specifics of the situation.

Following an episode of violence, there can be a variety of consequences for the victim, including physical injury, psychological trauma, loss of self-esteem and trust, social isolation, and other negative consequence[177].

The "honeymoon" phase. After the act of violence, there is a period of reconciliation known as the "honeymoon phase." During this time, the aggressor may feel guilt or shame and try to make amends by making apologies and promises to change. The victim may believe these promises and hope that the violence will not happen again. This phase may last for a while, but eventually tensions begin to build again and the cycle of violence repeats itself.

The justification or honeymoon period can manifest in various ways:

---

[174] Psychological Violence
[175] Sexual Violence
[176] Economic Violence
[177] Consequences of Domestic Violence

- Apologies and promises to change: The abuser may offer apologies and statements about his negative actions. He may promise to change, to be a better partner and to stop the violence. These apologies and promises may be sincere or may be used as a means of control or manipulation[178].
- Pleasant Moments and Conflict Resolution: In this phase, the abuser may actively create pleasant moments and attempt to resolve conflicts in the relationship. He may show care, attention, and engage in romantic or loving activities to restore harmony and balance in the relationship[179].
- Promises of professional help: The abuser may offer to go to counseling or therapy to address relationship problems and abuse. He may promise to get professional help and work on his problems or the causes of the abuse[180].
- Influencing emotional dependency: The abuser may use the victim's emotional dependency and her fear of losing the relationship to keep her close to him. He may manipulate her feelings by making it seem that only he can give her love, care, or security[181].
- During the period of justification and reconsolidation, the abuser may try to mitigate the negative effects of the violent episode, maintain control over the victim, and continue the relationship. The victim may feel mixed emotions, hopes for change[182].
- Hiding the violence from the outside world: The abuser may try to keep the domestic violence a secret and avoid detection or interference from outside persons such as family, friends,

---

[178] Book 13: Communicating with your partner. Manipulation. Conflict Management. Control, Manipulation
[179] Book 11: The Science of Relationships: love, partnership, harmony in a couple. Rose and Barbed Wire Theory
[180] Book 12: Motives for Marriage: Sex, Family, Parenting, Money. Family Therapy
[181] Book 2: Emotions and reason: keys to understanding relationships. Emotional Intelligence
[182] Book 7: The logic of love: thinking in relationships. Attitudes - Beliefs

neighbors, or law enforcement. He may convince the victim that their problems should remain within the family, that violence is a normal part of a relationship, or that no one will believe the victim. This is facilitated by the cultural stereotype of "keeping a low profile"[183].

It is important to note that the justification and reconciliation phase is not a sign of real change on the part of the abuser or a true reconciliation phase in the relationship. It is part of the cycle of abuse where the abuser uses various tactics to maintain control over the victim and continue the abuse. This can be difficult for the victim, as moments of caring and well-being can create the illusion that the abuse is over or that the relationship can be mended.

The lull phase - is a temporary period of no overt conflict or violence in the relationship. During this time, partners may feel relief and hope for positive change in the relationship. The relationship seems to be back to normal.

The lull in the cycle of violence can be deceptive, as the partner exhibiting violent behavior may use this time to manipulate and exert control over the victim. Instead of addressing underlying issues and triggers, the abuser may pretend as if nothing has happened and give the relationship the appearance of normalcy[184].

The partner who exhibits violent behavior may use the lull to apologize and promise to change. He or she may express regret, show remorse, and promise that similar situations will not happen again. The abuser may show increased interest and concern for the victim during the lull. He may be especially romantic, generous, and caring.

The victim may at this time hope for positive change in the relationship and believe in the sincerity of the partner. The victim may feel a great

---

[183] Book 9: Culture of love: norms, power, ethics. Culture of Silence, Stereotypes, Social Constructivism
[184] Book 6: Developmental level. Maturity of the partner. Maturity, Perception Filters, Lies

deal of power over the partner at this time. The roles of victim and aggressor may switch[185].

The abuser may then begin to increase his dominance, reestablish patterns of control, and suppress the victim's desire to express his needs or to contradict[186].

The cycle of violence will then repeat itself.

Unfortunately, in many cases, this cycle of violence continues until the victim decides to break the relationship with the aggressor or until action is taken to prevent the violence. It is important to recognize this cycle and if it is not possible to break it on your own, seek professional help to break it and get out of the toxic relationship[187].

The Narcissistic Abuse Cycle

In general, the cycle of narcissistic abusive behavior is the same as the cycle of abuse described above.

The narcissistic abusive cycle is a pattern of behavior that often occurs in relationships where one partner is a narcissist and the other is the victim of his or her abusive behavior[188].

The cycle consists of four main stages:

1. Idealization: the narcissist begins his relationship with the victim by admiring and emphasizing her qualities. The narcissist creates an idealized image and loves and honors the victim.
2. Destruction: after the victim becomes dependent on the narcissist and begins to rely on his or her support, the narcissist begins to reveal his or her flaws and exhibit abusive

---

[185] Book 11: The Science of Relationships: love, partnership, harmony in a couple. Karpman Triangle
[186] Book 9: Culture of love: norms, power, ethics. Power, Control
[187] Toxicity
[188] Book 3: The Psychology of Relationships: Traumas, Defenses, Behavioral Styles. Personality Disorders - Narcissistic Personality Disorder

behavior. The narcissist may criticize, insult, humiliate, neglect the victim, and exhibit other forms of psychological abuse.
3. Denial: when the victim begins to protest the abusive behavior, the narcissist begins to deny its existence or guilt. He may shift the blame to the victim, say that it is the victim's own fault for the abusive behavior, or deny its existence altogether.
4. Cyclical repetition: after the narcissist denies blame or the existence of the abusive behavior, the cycle begins again. The narcissist falls back into idealizing the victim to create an image of the perfect significant other and starts the cycle of abusive behavior all over again.

This cycle can repeat itself many times, resulting in emotional and psychological trauma for the victim. It is important to realize that narcissistic abusive behavior is a serious form of psychological abuse and requires professional help to overcome it.

Habituation (addiction)

In the context of abusive behavior and the cycle of violence, habituation (addiction) can find its application. Habituation in this case may involve the victim gradually becoming accustomed to the violent behavior of their partner. At the beginning of the relationship, the violence may be absent or negligible, but over time and repeated situations of violence, the victim may gradually become accustomed to the behavior[189].

The habituation process in the cycle of violence may manifest itself in this way: a gradual decrease in the victim's response to violence as a result of continued or repeated stimulation in the relationship. Initially, the violence may cause the victim to react strongly and be shocked, but over time and repetition of violent acts, the victim may become accustomed to the behavior and its intensity may diminish. This can

---

[189] Book 3: The Psychology of Relationships: Traumas, Defenses, Behavioral Styles. Milgram Experiment

happen either consciously, when the victim tries to adapt to the situation, or unconsciously.

It is important to note that habituation in the context of violence does not mean that the victim approves or agrees with the violence. Rather, it is a mental process where the victim may become habituated to the violence in an attempt to adapt to an unpleasant situation or to avoid more serious consequences[190].

The opposite of habituation in this context is unlearning. Unlearning can occur when altered but similar violent behavior elicits a response in the victim. However, it should be noted that the process of habituation and unlearning does not interrupt the cycle of violence but is part of a continuum that can accompany violence in relationships.

Intimate Partner Violence

Intimate partner violence is a form of violence between partners that may include physical violence, psychological violence, sexual violence, economic violence, and/or social isolation[191].

This violence can be either a one-time event or a recurring event. Both men and women can be victims of intimate partner violence, but in most cases, women are the victims.

Violence in intimate relationships can have the following forms of expression:

- Physical aggression towards the partner, which can be manifested by acts of beating, hitting, slapping and kicking.
- Coercion for sexual contact.
- Psychological abuse, such as constant humiliation or intimidation.
- Controlling a partner (directing actions, restricting contact with family and friends).

---

[190] Book 13: Communicating with your partner. Manipulation. Conflict Management. Cognitive Dissonance Theory
[191] Vocabulary of Violence

The term "domestic violence" and "intimate partner violence" are used interchangeably because both describe a form of violence that occurs within an intimate or family relationship. However, the term 'domestic violence' may be broader and include violence not only between intimate partners, but also violence between relatives, including children and parents, siblings, and between relatives and cohabitants[192].

In the context of violence in family relationships, four types of psychological violence must be distinguished: humiliation and damage to self-esteem, passive-aggressive withdrawal of emotional support, threats and restriction of personal freedom and territory:

- Denigrating Damage refers to a situation in which a person uses verbal aggression, such as yelling at his or her partner with obscene and demeaning language.
- Passive Aggressive Withholding of Emotional Support refers to the behavior of a person who intentionally avoids and withdraws from their partner in an effort to be dismissive and emotionally rejecting.
- Threatening Behavior refers to a situation where a person makes verbal threats to their partner that may involve physical harm, threats of divorce, lying, and threats of reckless behavior that could jeopardize their safety.
- Restricting Personal Territory and Freedom refers to isolating social support from family and friends. It can include taking away a partner's autonomy and lack of personal boundaries.

These types are discussed in more detail in the Domestic Violence section.

Intimate Terrorism or Coercive Control

The most extreme type of violence within intimate partner relationships is called intimate terrorism or coercive control. In this

---

[192] Domestic Violence

situation, one partner systematically displays violence and control over the other[193].

Intimate terrorism is an extreme form of intimate partner violence where one partner systematically exhibits control and violence over the other partner.

It is an extreme type of domestic violence that can include physical, emotional, psychological and sexual abuse, as well as financial control, isolation and threats.

Intimate terrorism is more likely to escalate over time, is unlikely to be mutual, and is more likely to result in serious injury. Victims of one type of violence often become victims of other types of violence. Severity tends to increase when there are multiple incidents, especially if the violence occurs in many forms.

It is most often perpetrated by men and requires medical attention and the use of women's shelters. Different forms of self-defense and psychological training are available to counteract this type of violence[194].

Studies of domestic violence among men show that they are less likely to report violence perpetrated by their intimate partner[195].

Women are more likely to engage in violent acts in retaliation or self-defense. They resort to less serious forms of violence than men, while men are more prone to long cycles of violence than women[196].

Situation Violence

Situational violence is a form of violence in intimate partner relationships that includes various forms of physical, emotional and psychological aggression that manifest themselves in response to specific situations or events in the relationship[197].

---

[193] Control
[194] Conflict Management
[195] Sexual Violence
[196] Cycle of violence

Situational violence often occurs during quarrels and conflicts between partners and can be both physical and verbal in nature. Unlike intimate terrorism, situational violence is not an attempt to control a partner, but rather is an expression of emotion, anger, and frustration[198].

Situational couple violence occurs with equal frequency by men and women, rarely results in serious injury, and is not a means of controlling a partner. It involves moderately aggressive behavior such as throwing objects, pushing, biting, hitting, etc.[199]

Situational violence in couples includes:

- Mode: moderately aggressive behavior. From throwing objects, to more aggressive behavior such as pushing, slapping, biting, hitting, scratching, or pulling hair.
- Frequency: less frequent than partner terrorism. Occurs occasionally during an argument or disagreement.
- Severity: milder than intimate terrorism. Very rarely escalates to more serious violence, usually does not involve serious injury or injuries that resulted in hospitalization of one partner.
- Reciprocity: Violence can be equally manifested by either partner in the relationship.
- Intent: Occurs out of anger or frustration, rather than as a means of gaining control and power over the other partner[200].

A 2010 survey found that common motivations for women taking male IPV were anger, a need for attention, or a reaction to their partner's violence.

IPV is an acronym that stands for "Intimate Partner Violence.".

A 2011 review published in the Journal of Aggression and Violence found differences in the methods of abuse used by men and women.

---

[197] Aggression and Violence
[198] Interpersonal Conflict
[199] Physical Violence
[200] Book 2: Emotions and reason: keys to understanding relationships. Emotional self-regulation

Men were more likely to beat or choke their partners, while women were more likely to "throw something at their partner, slap, kick, bite, hit with a fist or any object"

Population-based surveys based on victim reports provide the most accurate estimates of the prevalence of intimate partner violence and sexual violence in non-conflict settings. A WHO study in 10 predominantly developing countries found that among women aged 15 to 49 years, between 15% (Japan) and 70% (Ethiopia and Peru) of women reported physical and/or sexual intimate partner violence.

Intimate partner violence and sexual violence have serious short- and long-term physical, mental, sexual and reproductive health problems for victims and their children and result in high social and economic costs. These include both fatal and non-fatal injuries, depression and post-traumatic stress disorder, unwanted pregnancies, and sexually transmitted diseases including HIV. For more information on types of violence between partners, see the section on domestic violence[201].

Domestic violence

Domestic violence, or abusive behavior, is defined as chronic abuse in marriage, family, dating and other intimate, including romantic, relationships. It can include emotionally abusive behavior, humiliation, physical and sexual abuse, and other forms[202].

When people think of a victim of domestic violence, they immediately picture a woman. And it is true that the injuries suffered by female victims of domestic violence tend to be more severe than those suffered by male victims, and that violence by men is likely to be more frequent and severe.

***Domestic violence** is violence or other abuse that occurs in a domestic setting, such as marriage or cohabitation.*

---

[201] Sexual Violence
[202] Abuse

However, men are also often victims of domestic violence. A recent survey of British adults found that about 40% of victims of domestic violence are male. One nationwide survey in the United States found that 12.1% of women and 11.3% of men reported that they had committed an act of violence against their spouse in the past year.

Other studies have shown that women are just as likely as men to initiate violent confrontations with their spouses. The stereotype that men cannot be victims of domestic violence and fears of stigmatization often prevent men from reporting violence or seeking help[203].

Domestic violence can be called intimate partner violence when it is committed by a spouse or partner in an intimate relationship against another spouse or partner[204].

Domestic violence, *also family violence, is violence or mistreatment of one person against another committed in a domestic setting, such as marriage or cohabitation.*

It can also include violence against children, parents, or the elderly.

Domestic violence is not a mere quarrel or family conflict.

Conflict in a family implies an equal position of spouses or partners who do not agree on something and have the right to express their opinion[205].

In a situation of violence, one person seeks to control the other by using their physical strength, economic power, social status, etc.[206].

Abuse is distinguished from quarrel or conflict by the methodical and repetitiveness of acts of aggression. While conflict in the family is

---

[203] Psychological Violence
[204] Intimate Partner Violence
[205] Book 13: Communicating with your partner. Manipulation. Conflict Management. Causes of Conflict, Partnership
[206] Typology of Violence

always an isolated episode, violence is a carefully constructed system[207].

Domestic violence can occur in both heterosexual and homosexual relationships, as well as toward former spouses or partners. It is often stated that abusive behavior is intended to gain power and control over the victim. It can take the form of physical, verbal, religious, reproductive, psychological, economic, and sexual abuse, which can range from barely recognizable coercive forms to marital rape and physical violence such as choking, beating, etc.[208].

There is a perception that domestic violence is symmetrically gendered, but the level of harm caused can vary.

Research shows that women are more likely to use violence in self-defense, but there are also cases of women committing physical violence against their partners. In some countries, domestic violence may be justified by law, especially in cases of perceived or actual infidelity on the part of the woman[209].

The level of gender equality in a country can influence the level of domestic violence, with countries with less gender equality having higher levels of domestic violence. The incidence of domestic violence does not depend on the sexual orientation of the partners, and it can occur in both same-sex and opposite-sex relationships.

Causes of domestic violence may be related to the abuser's belief that violence is acceptable and justified or that the violence will not be reported to outsiders[210].

---

[207] Family System, Cycle of Violence
[208] Book 13: Communicating with your partner. Manipulation. Conflict Management.
[209] Physical Violence
[210] Book 7: The logic of love: thinking in relationships. Culture, Attitudes, Maladaptive schemas, Worldview

The main factors that can contribute to domestic violence are:

Upbringing and family experiences: Adults who witnessed violence in their families or were exposed to it themselves as children may replicate these negative behaviors in their own relationships[211].

Cultural and social factors: In some cultures, and societies, violence may be acceptable or even supported, creating an environment for domestic violence[212].

Inadequate anger and stress management: People who have poorly developed anger and stress management skills may use violence as a way to cope with negative emotions and conflict[213].

Mental and emotional problems: Certain mental health disorders, such as depression, anxiety disorders, personality disorders, or addictions, increase the likelihood of aggressive behavior and violence[214].

Inequality and patriarchal structures: In relationships where one partner dominates and controls the other, the possibility of domestic violence increases[215].

Economic and social stresses: Poverty, unemployment, poor education, and social isolation can contribute to domestic violence[216].

Low self-esteem and insecurity: People with low self-esteem and insecurity may use violence to assert themselves and maintain control over their partner[217].

---

[211] Book 12: Motives for Marriage: Sex, Family, Parenting, Money. Parenting
[212] Book 9: Culture of love: norms, power, ethics. Culture
[213] Book 2: Emotions and reason: keys to understanding relationships. Emotional Self-Regulation
[214] Book 3: The Psychology of Relationships: Traumas, Defenses, Behavioral Styles. Mental Disorders
[215] Book 11: The Science of Relationships: love, partnership, harmony in a couple. Patriarchy
[216] Book 12: Motives for Marriage: Sex, Family, Parenting, Money. Budget
[217] Book 3: The Psychology of Relationships: Traumas, Defenses, Behavioral Styles. Self-concept

Lack of empathy and sense of superiority: Individuals who lack empathy and often see themselves as superior to others may engage in aggressive and violent behavior to bend their partner to their will[218].

Violent Learning: In some cases, individuals may be taught violence through the media, video games, or their peers, which can lead to the transfer of this behavior into personal relationships.

Violent tendencies: Some individuals may have increased tendencies toward cruelty and aggression, which can lead to domestic violence[219].

Desire for revenge: In some cases, domestic violence may result from a desire for revenge for previous offenses, real or imagined.

Victims may resist violence, but it can be difficult to draw the line between self-defense and retaliation. The higher the partner's level of self-development and education, the more adequate their partner is, as the consequences of non-legal behavior will lead to retaliatory violence on behalf of the state[220].

Abuse
Abuse and domestic violence are often used synonymously.

In general, abusive relationships is a broader term that includes domestic violence as well as other forms of adverse or harmful behavior in the family environment.

An abusive relationship is a relationship in which the partner violates the other person's personal boundaries, humiliates, and tolerates cruelty in communication and actions in order to suppress the will of the victim.

In this type of relationship, the victim and the aggressor do not change places. The victim, for some reason, cannot get out of this relationship.

---

[218] Book 2: Emotions and reason: keys to understanding relationships. Empathy
[219] Aggression
[220] Book 9: Culture of love: norms, power, ethics. State, Level of Development

Both men and women can act as abusers, one difference is that each of them negatively affects their partner in different ways[221].

In an abusive relationship, one party (the abuser) uses their power and control over the other party (the victim) to dominate, subjugate, or cause harm. The victim may experience fear, anxiety, helplessness, low self-esteem, and other negative emotions[222].

Abusive relationships are dysfunctional, unequal, and harmful relationships between people that are characterized by systematic forms of violence, control, manipulation, and oppression. They can manifest in various areas of life, including familial, romantic, friendship, or professional relationships.

Recall that the higher the level of gender equality - the less violence[223].

Abusive relationships can take many forms, including physical abuse, emotional and psychological abuse, sexual abuse, financial abuse, social isolation, control and manipulation. Characteristics of abusive relationships include inequalities of power and control, violations of boundaries and personal autonomy, and recurring cycles of violence and manipulation[224].

---

[221] Book 10: Choosing the ideal partner. Masculinity and femininity. Boundaries, Co-dependency
[222] Book 11: The Science of Relationships: love, partnership, harmony in a couple. Control, Feelings, Object Relations Theory
[223] Book 10: Choosing the ideal partner. Masculinity and femininity. Gender
[224] see Cycle of Violence, Manipulation

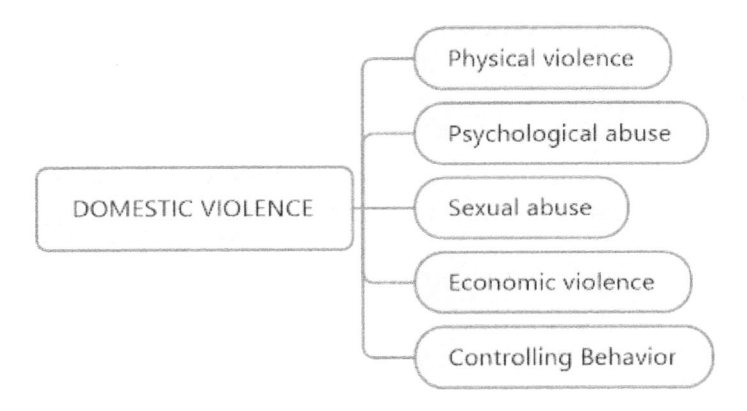

```
                         ┌── Physical violence
                         │
                         ├── Psychological abuse
                         │
DOMESTIC VIOLENCE ───────┼── Sexual abuse
                         │
                         ├── Economic violence
                         │
                         └── Controlling Behavior
```

The following types of domestic violence (abusive behavior) are distinguished:

- Physical - beating, pushing, slapping, throwing, strangling, burning (20%)
- Sexual - coercion through threats, blackmail, force (23%)
- Psychological/emotional - humiliation of honor, dignity, personality, emotional contamination, threats, intimidation, blackmailing children, scandal, yelling. 50+%
- Economic - manipulation of money, resources 50+%
- Restriction of freedom - locked in apartments, cars, threat to kick out of the house 10%.

Percentages in brackets show the frequency of manifestations and can vary depending on the country and socio-economic factors. But in any case, abusive behavior remains a serious problem worldwide that requires attention and measures to prevent and reduce its impact on victims and society as a whole[225].

Culture has a significant impact on the prevalence of domestic violence.

---

[225] Book 9: Culture of love: norms, power, ethics. Human Rights

This is shown by the statistics of violence in different cultures.

Individualistic cultures:

- Physical violence: 15-25% on average
- Psychological violence: 35-50% on average
- Sexual violence: 3-10% on average
- Economic violence: 10-20% on average
- Controlling behavior: 30-40% on average

In collectivist cultures:

- Physical violence: average 20-35%
- Psychological violence: average 45-60%
- Sexual violence: average 5-15%
- Economic violence: average 15-25%
- Controlling behavior: average 40-50%

It is worth noting that these figures are general trends and may vary from country to country and culturally. In addition, violence can manifest itself in different forms and its impact can vary depending on the specific situation and the characteristics of the victim and the abuser[226].

Let's look at how current theories justify domestic violence.

The evolutionary-biological explanation of domestic violence claims that it is a way for men to control female reproduction and ensure their sexual exclusivity. In some parts of the world, violence associated with extramarital relationships is considered justified. For example, in a survey in Turkey, 37% of respondents said that a woman who commits adultery should be killed, while 21% said her nose or ears should be cut off[227].

---

[226] Book 11: The Science of Relationships: love, partnership, harmony in a couple. Leary Test
[227] Book 10: Choosing the ideal partner. Masculinity and femininity. Social Constructivism

Psychological theories focus on personality traits and mental characteristics of the offender. Personality traits include sudden outbursts of anger, poor impulse control, and low self-esteem. Violence experienced in childhood causes some people to become more violent as adults. A correlation has been found between juvenile delinquency and domestic violence in adulthood[228].

Social theories describe external factors in the offender's environment, such as family structure, stress, and social learning, and include rational choice theories. Social learning theory suggests that people learn by observing and copying the behavior of others, and if that behavior receives positive feedback, it continues. If the antisocial behavior does not receive negative feedback, it is more likely to continue[229].

Economic theories. Resource theory was developed by William Hood in 1971. Women who depend on their husbands for economic support (e.g., homemakers, women with disabilities, unemployed women) often fear that separating from their husbands will increase their financial burdens and therefore have fewer coping options and resources[230].

Power. Couples who have an equal distribution of power are less prone to conflict, and if conflict does occur, they are less likely to be violent. However, if one spouse seeks control and power in the relationship, this can lead to violence, including intimidation, emotional and economic abuse, isolation, and the use of children. In some cases, perpetrators of domestic violence may see themselves as victims; because of their anger and difficulties in communicating with their partners, they psychologically force themselves to see themselves as victims[231].

---

[228] Book 3: The Psychology of Relationships: Traumas, Defenses, Behavioral Styles. Mental Disorders
[229] Book 12: Motives for Marriage: Sex, Family, Parenting, Money. Parenting
[230] Economic Violence
[231] Emotional Self-Regulation, Shaping Conflict

Control

Control can manifest itself as both internal control (self-control) and external control (control by a partner or other people).

Control is the process of regulating behavior or a situation in accordance with given norms, standards, or goals.

Control can be beneficial to a person if it allows him or her to manage his or her behavior and achieve his or her goals. However, too strict or excessive control can lead to negative consequences such as feelings of helplessness, low self-esteem, anxiety, depression, or maladjustment. In such cases, it is important to find a balance between control and freedom that is in line with individual needs and goals[232].

The distinction between caring and controlling is quite fine[233].

When they start telling you what to do, this is obvious control. This behavior in a relationship indicates that one partner considers the other to be un-self-sufficient. In other words, it is a manifestation of distrust in the partner[234]. Let me remind you that trust, along with respect, is one of the key factors in a happy relationship[235].

Controlling behavior

Manipulators and abusers may use a variety of methods to control their victims, such as positive and negative reinforcement, psychological punishment, and traumatic tactics, including insults and rage[236].

---

[232] Book 8: Harmony of personality: self-esteem in relationships. Harmony
[233] Book 11: The Science of Relationships: love, partnership, harmony in a couple. Harmony in Couples
[234] Book 9: Culture of love: norms, power, ethics. Patriarchy - Principles of Patriarchy in Modern Relationships
[235] Book 11: The Science of Relationships: love, partnership, harmony in a couple. Partnership - Trust
[236] Intimate Partner Violence

Controlling behavior is when one person attempts to manage, limit, or control another person, often by imposing his or her views, values, and preferences.

Controlling behavior can come in many forms, such as manipulation, criticism, pressure, violence, or threats[237].

Controlling behavior can be harmful to another person's autonomy, self-esteem, and emotional well-being because it undermines their ability to make their own decisions and choose the life they want[238].

Frequent cycles of abuse can create a traumatic bond and an atmosphere of fear between the abuser and victim. Victims may attempt to normalize or justify negative behaviors, sometimes even blaming themselves[239].

Research suggests that some personality disorders may be associated with a propensity for violence, especially if the person suffered from a traumatic childhood[240].

Key signs of controlling behavior include:

- Excessive interference in another person's private life.
- Constant criticism or humiliation.
- Manipulation, through guilt, fear or responsibility.
- Isolation from friends, family, and social networks.
- Restricting access to resources such as money, education, or medical care.
- Monitoring or controlling communication and movements.
- Threats or acts of violence to increase control.

Power, control, and violence

---

[237] Vocabulary of Violence
[238] Book 8: Harmony of personality: self-esteem in relationships. Self-Esteem
[239] Book 11: The Science of Relationships: love, partnership, harmony in a couple. Co-dependency, Cycle of Abuse
[240] Personality Disorders, Aggression, Parenting, Psychological Trauma

The logic of control can be explained through the immaturity, irresponsibility and/or consumerist attitude of one of the partners[241].

Responsibility is the obligation to fulfill one's duties and bear the consequences of one's actions and decisions.

When one of the partners does not want or cannot extract resources himself, does not take responsibility for himself and his actions, he thus goes into a childish position, shifts all responsibility to the partner, gives him the power and right to make decisions[242].

The partner who extracts resources knows their price better, sees the future further, tries to prevent a crisis. He carries the financial burden and in order to compensate for the psychological balance, automatically goes into an adult position[243].

Now he alone provides financial security and stability of the couple's life. As a consequence, the responsible partner is forced to control the irresponsible partner, because the latter becomes irrational, shortsighted, uncritical of himself and the world, irresponsible. His "want" is more important than "can" and "must"[244].

Such control generates violence.

At first mild, in the form of sanctions, restrictions and beliefs, then more severe - turning into abusive behavior, manipulation and blackmail[245].

---

[241] Book 5: How to find happiness: looking through the window of the world picture. Consumer Society, Human Rights
[242] Book 6: Developmental level. Maturity of the partner. Maturity, Patriarchy - Principles of Patriarchy in Modern Relationships
[243] Book 9: Culture of love: norms, power, ethics. Family System
[244] Book 1: The biology of relationships: why people form couples. Biopsychosocial Structure of Personality, Expectations from Partner, Gender Stereotypes, Co-dependency
[245] Book 10: Choosing the ideal partner. Masculinity and femininity. Manipulation, Patriarchy - The Provider Model

Over time, the child's position strengthens as the person becomes more aware of the secondary benefits of this position. He changes behavior, completely resembling the baby: I want this, buy that, do this, do that, etc. This behavior is based on irresponsibility. Lack of responsibility corrupts the personality, and the partner becomes lazy in other aspects of the relationship[246].

The value of such a partner in the eyes of the other person is sharply reduced.

The life position of the immature partner, becomes shallower and more insignificant for the second partner. After time comes the stage of accumulation of claims. The skewed take-give balance reaches a critical point, followed by devaluation and the collapse of the relationship. This is just one of the scenarios of controlling behavior[247].

Control is one of the basic functions of a control system. Control is carried out on the basis of observing the behavior of the controlled system in order to ensure optimal functioning of the latter (measuring the achieved results and correlating them with the expected results). On the basis of control data, the system is adapted, i.e. optimizing management decisions are made.

Control in the family is often a consequence of gender identity, where the partner living in a weak and irresponsible position (more often women) allows themselves actions that negatively affect family life. This forces the mature partner to incorporate elements of control into their life[248].

Control in relationships is a common problem.

According to a 2011 American survey, nearly 70% of women have experienced displays of control and almost 40% were exclusively in a

---

[246] Causes of Conflicts, Partnership - Responsibility, Three-Component Theory of Love
[247] Book 11: The Science of Relationships: love, partnership, harmony in a couple. Take-Give Balance, Stages of Relationship Development, Defense Mechanisms, Divorce, Karpman's Triangle
[248] Book 10: Choosing the ideal partner. Masculinity and femininity. Gender Identity, Leadership

partner-controlled relationship. In the UK, according to 2018 data, nearly a third of the population has been in this type of relationship - and women are nearly one and a half times less likely to exhibit controlling behavior than men. Which is explained by the breadwinner model inherent in patriarchal relationships[249].

Recall the psychological defense of omnipotent control that explains aggressor behavior:

Omnipotent control *is a mental process attributed to psychological defense mechanisms. It consists in a person's unconscious conviction that he is able to control everything.*

The natural consequence of this conviction is a person's feeling of responsibility for everything around him and the feeling of guilt that arises if something is out of his control. This forms hyper-responsibility[250].

Hyper-responsibility

Hyper-responsibility can manifest itself in excessive concern for others, constant feelings of guilt and worry, even when there is no real reason for it.

Hyper-responsibility is a condition in which a person experiences too much responsibility for their own actions as well as the actions of others.

People who suffer from hyper-responsibility can often feel intense anxiety when something doesn't go according to plan or when they feel that they haven't fulfilled their responsibilities one hundred percent. Hyper-responsibility can lead to excessive fatigue, stress, anxiety, and depression, so it is important to learn how to cope with this condition.

---

[249] Book 12: Motives for Marriage: Sex, Family, Parenting, Money. Patriarchy, Social Constructivism
[250] Book 3: The Psychology of Relationships: Traumas, Defenses, Behavioral Styles. Defense Mechanisms

The main cause of hyper-responsibility is a lack of understanding of one's boundaries: where I am, where mine is, where the other person and their boundaries begin, which is the main cause of abusive behavior[251].

Hyper-responsibility is the basis of controlling behavior[252].

This is how a seemingly positive quality (responsibility) is linked to a negative phenomenon - partner control.

Types and forms of controlling behavior:

Controlling behavior can manifest itself in different forms and at different levels:

- Physical controlling behavior: this may include threats, violence, coercion and restraint.
- Emotional controlling behavior: this may include criticism, blaming, ignoring, isolation and manipulation.
- Financial controlling behavior: this may include controlling a partner's finances, setting limits on spending, banning them from work, threatening to take away their livelihood, etc.
- Social controlling behavior: this may include controlling the partner's social life, prohibiting contact with friends and family, establishing control over phone calls and messages, etc.
- Sexual controlling behavior: this may include forcing sexual acts that are not desirable to the partner, threatening to disclose intimate information, etc.
- Behavioral control: this may include setting rules and restrictions on a partner's behavior, such as prohibiting certain actions, setting schedules, etc.
- Thought control: this may include controlling your partner's thoughts and emotions, establishing certain beliefs, ignoring feelings, etc.

---

[251] Abuse
[252] Book 11: The Science of Relationships: love, partnership, harmony in a couple. Co-dependency

- Appearance control: this may include controlling a partner's appearance, setting requirements for clothing, hairstyle, etc.

Some forms of controlling behavior have been given separate names - neglect, isolation, control, restraint and isolation[253].

Controlling behavior can manifest itself in many different ways and at many different levels and can be highly harmful to the health and well-being of partners[254].

Partner Control

Control by the romantic partner can manifest as positive (caring, attention, support) or negative (control, manipulation, abusive, violent).

- Positive control by the partner can be constructive and help establish a stable relationship, however, excessive control can lead to feelings of pressure, which can lead to negative consequences.
- Negative control from a romantic partner can come in the form of violence or manipulation, which can lead to a deterioration of the relationship and psychological or physical abuse. This can be especially dangerous if the partner is under the delusion that control is a sign of love and caring.

Excessive control can lead to one partner becoming less independent and dependent on the other. In such a situation, an imbalance of power can occur, which can lead to one partner experiencing inequality or injustice[255].

---

[253] Vocabulary of Violence
[254] Intimate Partner Violence
[255] Book 11: The Science of Relationships: love, partnership, harmony in a couple. Object Relations Theory

It is important to realize that there should be respectful and mutual control in a relationship in which both partners have freedom of choice and autonomy[256].

Mutual control should be constructive and focused on achieving common goals and interests[257].

Examples of positive controlling behavior:

- Reminding you of important things to do
- Helping you solve problems and make decisions
- Support in difficult situations
- Help with time management and planning
- Supporting personal growth and development
- Providing assistance with tasks

Examples of negative controlling behaviors:

- Prohibiting socializing with friends and family
- Monitoring and managing your partner's finances
- Threats to break up
- Judging the partner and criticizing his or her actions
- Forcing sexual acts that are not desirable to the partner
- Criticizing a partner's appearance and clothing
- Prohibiting participation in activities and classes

It is crucial to remember that even positive controlling behavior can become excessive if it occurs too frequently or without the other partner's consent. Any controlling behavior should be based on trust and mutual agreement to avoid violating the rights of the other person[258].

---

[256] Book 10: Choosing the ideal partner. Masculinity and femininity. Partnership
[257] Book 11: The Science of Relationships: love, partnership, harmony in a couple. Boundaries
[258] Book 11: The Science of Relationships: love, partnership, harmony in a couple. Couple Harmony

Psychological Pressure

Psychological partner pressure is a form of negative control in which one partner uses manipulative and threatening tactics to control the behavior, thoughts, and feelings of the other partner. This can occur either consciously or unconsciously and can be one of the signs of emotional or psychological abuse[259].

Psychological pressure tactics may include the following:

- Using threats and blackmail to get desired behavior from the other partner.
- Criticizing and judging the other partner for their actions and behavior.
- Using flattery and praise to make the other partner feel indebted and submissive.
- Isolating the other partner from their friends, family and social network to create dependency and control over them.
- Suppressing the other partner's opinions and feelings to make them feel lesser or helpless.
- Using the threat of separation or loss of love to control the other partner's behavior

Psychological pressure on the partner can lead to feelings of helplessness, anxiety and depression in the victim, as well as deterioration of the relationship and breach of trust between partners.

Psychological pressure can also be either positive or negative.

Positive psychological pressure can be related to motivation, support, and assistance. Examples of positive psychological pressure include motivational words, support and assistance in solving problems.

Negative psychological pressure usually involves threatening, manipulating, and forcing another person to do something against

---

[259] Psychological abuse, Toxicity

their will. Examples of negative psychological pressure can be threats of separation, blackmail, confusion, etc.

Examples of positive psychological pressure:

- Motivating words and praise for efforts and achievements
- Support in difficult situations and help in solving problems
- Encouraging personal growth and development of the partner
- Facilitating the development of skills and abilities
- Providing constructive criticism to improve the relationship

Examples of negative psychological pressure:

- Threats to break up or pressure to stay in the relationship
- Blackmail and threats to harm your partner
- Using manipulation and deception to achieve their goals
- Using force and intimidation to get your partner to obey you
- Confusing or using emotional outbursts to get your way

It is important to remember that any psychological pressure on a partner must be based on respect, trust and consent of both parties to avoid violating the rights of the other person. Any form of pressure can lead to negative consequences in the relationship and should be used with caution[260].

Physical Violence

Physical violence is the easiest form of violence to understand.

Physical domestic violence is a global problem affecting millions of people every year. It creates fear, suffering and trauma, having a lasting impact on victims, their families and society as a whole.

Physical violence is the direct or indirect impact on the victim to cause physical harm, fear, pain, pain, injury, trauma, other physical suffering or bodily harm. In the context of coercive control, physical violence is the control of the victim.

---

[260] Book 11: The Science of Relationships: love, partnership, harmony in a couple. Partnership - Respect

Physical violence can be inflicted either once or systematically, in the family, community or work environment. It can lead to serious physical injury, mental health problems, and sometimes death.

For example, honor killing exists in some cultures.

Honor killing is a crime, the murder of a family member, most often (but not necessarily) female, committed by relatives for bringing shame (dishonor) upon the family

Physical domestic violence is a form of domestic violence in which one family member, usually a husband or father, uses violence against another family member, such as a wife, daughter, son, or older parents[261].

Physical violence is violence in which physical harm is inflicted on a person's body, including hitting, kicking, pushing, choking, forcible confinement, forced sedation, beatings and other forms of aggression that cause pain, injury, wounds or damage to the body.

Causes of physical violence in the family:

- Sociocultural factors: In some cultures, violence is seen as an acceptable way of resolving conflict or establishing power. Such attitudes may contribute to violence becoming the norm in family relationships.
- Stress and strain: Often family violence arises as a result of stress related to financial, professional or personal problems. Violence can be a way to cope with tension or to express anger and frustration.
- Learning Violence: Many abusers have witnessed or been victims of violence in their family as children. This can form behavioral patterns that are later passed on from generation to generation[262].

---

[261] Book 12: Motives for Marriage: Sex, Family, Parenting, Money. Family - Dysfunctional Family
[262] Book 3: The Psychology of Relationships: Traumas, Defenses, Behavioral Styles. Mental disorders

Physical domestic violence can have serious consequences for the victim, including physical and psychological trauma, constant fear and anxiety, health problems including heart disease and depression, and sometimes death. In addition, physical violence can affect other family members, including children, who may experience constant fear and anxiety and become victims of violence[263].

Physical violence in the family can manifest itself in a variety of ways:

- Punches and kicks. This is the most common form of physical violence in which the victim is hit in the face, body or head.
- Beating. This is a form of violence in which the victim is subjected to multiple blows that can cause serious injuries.
- Strangulation. This is a form of violence in which the abuser puts pressure on the victim's neck, which can lead to unconsciousness or even death.
- Partner restraint is a form of domestic violence in which one partner, using physical force, holds a partner in place.
- Violent Isolation. This is a form of violence in which the victim is forcibly confined in a room or house and cannot leave.
- Forced sedation. This is a form of violence in which the victim is forced to take medication that can cause unconsciousness or poisoning.

Each of these forms of physical violence can have different types and manifestations, depending on the specific situation and the personality of the abuser.

Physical violence is one of the most direct and obvious forms of aggression, in which the abuser uses physical force to cause pain, injury or damage to the victim's body[264].

Physical violence is the most legally elaborate form of violence. Most forms of physical domestic violence are punishable by law[265].

---

[263] Book 8: Harmony of personality: self-esteem in relationships. Parenting
[264] Aggression
[265] Legal Liability

The threat of physical violence is a form of psychological violence.

Psychological Violence

In contrast to physical violence, psychological violence, or domestic abuse, is a low-visibility but deeply destructive form of violence that can cause serious damage to the mental health and well-being of victims.

This type of violence is characteristic of situations of power imbalance, such as violent relationships, bullying, controlling behavior, and child abuse[266].

A number of countries provide for civil, administrative and criminal liability for psycho-emotional violence in its various forms. Depending on the consequences and circumstances, liability varies[267].

Psychological violence, also emotional or moral violence, is a form of violence that can lead to psychological trauma, including anxiety, depression and post-traumatic stress disorder.

In this formulation, there are three types of psychological violence - emotional, moral, and psychological violence itself[268].

Let's consider each of them:

- Emotional abuse: Emotional abuse manifests itself by using the victim's feelings and emotions against them in order to humiliate, dominate or control them. Examples of emotional abuse may include being ignored, neglected, humiliated, or remarks intended to invoke fear, shame, or guilt. Emotional abuse can also result in constant fluctuations between tenderness and cruelty, creating a state of anxiety and uncertainty for the victim.

---

[266] Control
[267] Legal Liability, Values
[268] Typology of Violence

- Moral abuse: Moral abuse involves the use of principles, values, or norms of behavior to manipulate, justify violence, or control the victim. This may take the form of manipulating the victim's sense of duty or responsibility, imposing stereotypes and restrictions, or demeaning the victim based on their cultural, religious or social affiliations. Moral violence may also include threats by the abuser to expose the victim or damage the victim's reputation.
- Psychological violence: Psychological violence, as a separate category, involves the use of manipulation, intimidation, coercion, lying or gaslighting to control and dominate the victim. It seeks to challenge doubts about one's own reality, narrow one's social circle, stifle self-expression, and exert control over the victim's life.

Although all three types of psychological abuse have their own characteristics, they are often closely intertwined and can complement each other, creating a toxic environment for the victim[269].

In general, psychological abuse can take many forms, including verbal abuse, constant criticism, intimidation, manipulation, or refusal to settle.

A partner, for example, constantly criticizes and demeans his or her partner, telling him or her that he or she will never be successful or is not good at his or her job. This is a form of psychological abuse that can lead to a decrease in the partner's self-esteem and self-worth, as well as cause anxiety and depression.

Psychological Violence and Relationships

Research suggests that psychological violence or aggression may be a causal factor in marital or relationship dissatisfaction. The study by Laurent et al. mentioned earlier reports that psychological aggression

---

[269] Toxicity

in young couples is associated with decreased satisfaction in both partners. This is because psychological aggression reflects less mature coercive tactics and an inability to effectively meet the needs of self and others[270].

In another study in 2008 focusing on relationship dissatisfaction among teenagers, Walsh and Shulman assert that women who display high levels of psychological aggression are less satisfied in their relationships, and this applies to both partners. It was also found that men's behavior expressed in the form of withdrawal, i.e., a less mature conflict resolution strategy, can lead to increased relationship satisfaction. In other words, emotional detachment is an unconscious response of men to toxic behavior from women and vice versa[271].

Men and Women

In general, women are more likely to use psychological violence and men more likely to use physical violence[272].

Psychological violence can be manifested and perceived differently by men and women. It is important to note that psychological violence is not limited to gender and can affect people of all genders and identities. Let us consider similarities and differences in the manifestation and perception of psychological violence in men and women.

Similarities:

- Manipulation and control: Both men and women can use manipulation and control to limit the victim's freedom, dictate behavior, and create a sense of powerlessness.

---

[270] Developmental Level, Toxicity
[271] Book 3: The Psychology of Relationships: Traumas, Defenses, Behavioral Styles. Defense Mechanisms
[272] Aggression - Men and Women, Violence and Gender, Violence and Level of Development

- Blame and Blaming: Both sexes may impose guilt and blame the victim for their problems in order to justify their behavior and strengthen their position.
- Ignoring and isolating: Men and women may neglect, ignore and cut off the victim's emotional needs in order to reinforce feelings of loneliness and dependency.

Differences:

- Aggression: Men are more likely to display psychological violence through overt aggression, such as yelling, threats, and outright defiance. Women may display aggression more covertly, through passive-aggressive behavior, manipulation, and scheming.
- Stereotypes and social expectations: Perceptions of psychological violence may be distorted by gender role stereotypes. Women may face additional misunderstanding and underestimation of their experiences because it is often assumed that violence can only be physical. Men, on the other hand, may face expectations of "being strong" and "not showing weakness", making it difficult to recognize and discuss psychological violence[273].
- Social support: Women often have more opportunities to discuss their experiences and receive support from friends, family and professionals, as society and social services have traditionally focused more on women as victims of violence. Men may find it difficult to seek support, which in turn can exacerbate their situation and lead to stigmatization[274].
- Influence of gender roles: Gender roles can influence how men and women manifest and perceive psychological violence. For example, women may be more likely to display violence through criticism and disparagement of appearance or

---

[273] Book 10: Choosing the ideal partner. Masculinity and femininity. Gender Stereotypes

[274] Book 10: Choosing the ideal partner. Masculinity and femininity. Femininity and Masculinity

domestic skills, whereas men may use violence to emphasize their dominance and control over finances or sexuality[275].
- Perceptions and Statistics: Psychological violence perpetrated by women may be underestimated or misinterpreted because society often assumes that women are less aggressive and dangerous than men. Male victims of psychological violence perpetrated by women may face misunderstanding and mistrust from others, making it difficult for them to get help and support[276].

Several studies have identified a double standard for emotional abuse by men and by women.

A double standard *is the application of different sets of principles to situations that are basically the same.*

According to a study by Follingstad and colleagues, even professional psychologists tend to view men's abuse of women in marriage as more serious compared to similar scenarios describing women's abuse of men. Similar to the link between physical aggression and men, there is a stereotypical link between psychological abuse and men, which, influences the evaluation of their actions[277].

Similarly, Sorenson and Taylor surveyed a randomly selected group of Los Angeles and California residents to investigate their views on hypothetical incidents of violence in heterosexual relationships. Their study found that violence perpetrated by women, including emotional and psychological violence such as control or humiliation, was generally viewed as less serious or destructive than similar violence by men[278].

---

[275] Social Constructivism, Aggression, Violence and Gender, Gender Conflict
[276] Book 10: Choosing the ideal partner. Masculinity and femininity. Gender Psychology
[277] Book 10: Choosing the ideal partner. Masculinity and femininity. Gender Psychology
[278] Violence and Gender

Culture

In collectivistic cultures, psychological violence is more prevalent than in individualistic cultures, but psychological violence often goes unreported and many cases may go unreported due to stigma, fear or lack of support for victims[279].

The patriarchy that dominates the world's cultures has contributed its correlates to how psychological violence from men and women is perceived. Existing patriarchal cultural norms, in which men are more dominant, suggest that men are more likely to abuse their partners. Therefore, male aggression is more harshly dealt with as early as adolescence. According to Walsh and Schluman, women grow up with fewer restrictions on aggressive behavior.

Hamel's 2007 study found that the "prevailing patriarchal view of intimate partner violence" has led to a systematic reluctance to study women who practice psychological violence.

Dutton found that male victims of violence are often blamed for their suffering. Victims of violence usually blame their behavior, not the abuser, and try to change to please it[280].

A 2002 study concluded that abusers seek complete control over various aspects of family life. This behavior is only sustained when the victim of abuse seeks to please the abuser[281].

Masochism-the tendency to derive pleasure through humiliation, violence, or torment.

Many abusers use manipulative techniques to control their victims, trying to persuade them to submit to their desires rather than forcing them to do things they do not want to do. According to Simon, psychological abuse can manifest itself subtly and covertly through various manipulation and control tactics. Victims often do not realize

---

[279] Book 10: Choosing the ideal partner. Masculinity and femininity. Gender Conflict - Sexism
[280] Victim blaming
[281] Control

the true nature of their relationship until conditions deteriorate significantly.

Strategies in Psychological Violence

The change in behavioral strategies to achieve a goal can be quite varied.

Stages of abusive (psychological) behavioral strategies:

- Aggression: Initially, an individual may use aggressive behavior to achieve his or her goals. However, if this does not produce the desired result, the individual may move on to the next strategy[282].
- Strategy Reset - "I was joking" or "you misunderstood": When realizing that aggressive behavior is ineffective, the individual may attempt to change his tactics by presenting his previous actions as a joke. In this way, he softens the perception of his aggressive behavior and shifts to softer strategies[283].
- Manipulation (underestimating the partner): If joking does not work, the individual may turn to manipulation, using the underestimation of the partner to achieve his or her goals. This may involve ignoring, neglecting, or deliberately underestimating the partner's merits and capabilities so that the partner doubts his or her abilities and is more controlling[284].
- A new strategy is persuasion (everyone does it): If manipulation also proven ineffective, the individual may turn to the strategy of persuasion, appealing to the norms of behavior or practices of the majority. Here he or she may argue that "everybody does it" so that the partner will succumb to social pressure to accept the proposed viewpoint or action[285].

---

[282] Toxicity
[283] Deception
[284] Manipulations

- Argumentation (peer communication): If the previous strategies have been unsuccessful, an individual may turn to argumentation, using logical and reasonable arguments to discuss with a partner as an equal. In this case, he or she seeks to achieve his or her goal through mutual understanding and agreement, which can be a more productive and respectful approach for both parties[286].

This same principle is applied to the destructive impact on a partner through manipulation or psychological violence. Often, after gaining control over the victim, the abuser prefers to isolate them, even resorting to physical restraint[287].

Portrait of a Psychological Abuser:

There is a major reason why people commit psychological violence - it is the desire for power and control over others[288].

Also, people who are prone to psychological violence can often be seen to have heightened suspicion and a tendency toward jealousy, lack of self-control, and a tendency toward aggression and justification of violence[289].

People who commit psychological and physical violence also often suffer from personality disorders[290].

It is not uncommon for abusers to try to avoid household chores or to completely control the family budget[291].

---

[285] Book 7: The logic of love: thinking in relationships. Attitudes, Dilts Pyramid, Perceptual Filters
[286] Book 13: Communicating with your partner. Manipulation. Conflict Management. Argumentation Theory, Graham's Pyramid
[287] Physical Violence
[288] Control
[289] Self-Knowledge, Aggression, Treason
[290] Book 3: The Psychology of Relationships: Traumas, Defenses, Behavioral Styles. Personality Disorders

They can also be very manipulative, trying to get the victim's friends and even relatives on their side and blaming the victim for their violence[292].

Characteristics of an Abuser:

- Low self-esteem: These people often doubt themselves and may depend on others' opinions for self-affirmation.
- Control: They seek to control others to maintain the illusion of their own importance and power.
- Volatility: Tendency to emotional outbursts and frequent mood swings.
- Manipulative: Use manipulation to achieve their goals and control others.

Motives:

- Desire for power and control: A sense of control over others is important to these individuals, which may be related to their own feelings of powerlessness.
- Self-assertion: Emotional violence may be a way of compensating for one's inferiority and suppressing one's weaknesses.
- Protection from vulnerability: Aggression and violence can be a defense mechanism against one's own vulnerability and fear of disclosure[293].

Goals:

- Subjugation of partner or others: These individuals seek to force others to conform to their needs by oppressing and suppressing them.

---

[291] Maturity, Economic Abuse
[292] Manipulation, Violence Lexicon
[293] Book 13: Communicating with your partner. Manipulation. Conflict Management. Communication with a partner

- Isolating the victim: Often tend to isolate the victim from friends and family in order to increase their control.
- Maintaining Power: A person prone to emotional abuse seeks to maintain their dominance in order to maintain their position in the relationship.

Instruments:

- Gaslighting: Manipulating facts and reality to make the victim doubt themselves and their perceptions.
- Threats and blackmail: Using threats and blackmail to make the victim obey and fear the consequences of disobedience.
- Blame and Blaming: Imposing guilt on the victim, blaming them for their own problems and failures.
- Silent Resistance: Ignoring the victim by not communicating with them or responding to their requests in order to create feelings of insecurity and isolation.
- Sarcasm and neglect: Insults, sarcasm and neglect of the victim can be used to humiliate and invoke feelings of inferiority.
- Economic abuse: Restricting or controlling the victim's access to financial resources to increase dependence on the abuser.
- Isolation: Restricting the victim's contact with friends and family, preventing the victim from participating in social events and creating dependency on the abuser.
- Control over daily life: Monitoring the victim, controlling where she goes, who she socializes with, what she wears, etc.

Emotional violence can manifest itself in different forms and in varying degrees of severity.

In most cases, psychological violence is felt in the body as an emotion and only later realized as a violation of rights, morality, justice and respect[294].

---

[294] Book 2: Emotions and reason: keys to understanding relationships. Emotions, Social Norms, Ethics, Kohlberg's Theory of Moral Development, Partnership - Respect

Terminology.

Let's pass along the terminology to make it easier for you to understand each situation:

- Verbal abuse is the use of threats, insults or swear words to another person. For example, constantly humiliating and insulting a partner.
- Criticizing and belittling - Criticizing and belittling statements to humiliate and lower another person's self-esteem. For example, continuous criticism of appearance or the way they show their feelings.
- Isolation from friends and family - Isolation from friends and family for the purpose of control and manipulation. For example, forbidding communication with friends and family or constantly controlling communication.
- Intimidation - Creating threats and fear to make another person obey. For example, threats of physical violence or divorce.
- Humiliation - Humiliating, insulting, and displaying low status in order to control and manipulate. For example, publicly insulting a partner or lashing out in front of friends or children.
- Threats - Threats of physical or psychological violence, for the purpose of control and manipulation. For example, threats of violence or suicide if the other person does not comply.
- Blaming - Placing blame on another person, even if they are not responsible. For example, blaming your partner for your own failures and problems[295].
- Silent treatment - Refusing to communicate with another person, without giving a reason. For example, refusing to answer calls or messages, or refusing to talk during a conflict.
- Withholding affection - Refusing to show love and affection to another person for the purpose of control and manipulation.

---

[295] Locus Control, Communicating with your partner - Sincerity

For example, refusing to make physical contact and show concern for a partner. Women often use "sex trafficking" as leverage to coerce a partner to their goal[296].

- Undermining self-esteem - Acts or words intended to humiliate and undermine another person's self-esteem. For example, criticizing another person's appearance and the way they show their feelings in order to lower their self-esteem[297].
- Manipulation - The use of various tactics to get a desired result from another person. For example, using promises and threats to get another person to comply with your demand[298].
- Cyberstalking - Using the internet and social media to control and manipulate another person. For example, constantly tracking your partner's location or constantly texting to control their actions.
- Using children as leverage - Using children as a means to gain a desired outcome or control over another person. For example, threatening to take the children away if your partner does not do what you want.
- Withholding information - refusing to give necessary information to another person in order to control the situation and manage their reaction. For example, refusing to tell the other person about your plans and actions in order to prevent the other person from making a decision based on that information[299].
- Coercion - Using force or threats to get the other person to do what you want. For example, threatening violence or threatening to hurt someone close to you to make your partner obey your demands.
- Unreasonable demands - Demands that are unreasonable or unrealistic yet insist on compliance. For example, demanding

---

[296] Sexual Abuse
[297] Self-esteem
[298] Manipulation
[299] Communicating with a Partner - Sincerity

constant monitoring of your partner's location or constantly criticizing and insulting him or her.
- Gaslighting - A form of manipulation in which one person convinces another person that their perception of reality is wrong in order to control their behavior. For example, convincing a partner that his or her doubts are unfounded and that he or she cannot trust his or her feelings.

Let's examine this form of psychological violence in more detail as it entails numerous nuances.

Gaslighting

Gaslighting is a term that has gained widespread recognition in recent years, although the practice itself has existed for much longer. This method of psychological manipulation involves making a person doubt their own reality, memory, or judgments. In other words, gaslighting is a denial of the adequacy of reality to the partner[300].

The term "gaslighting" originates from Patrick Hamilton's play "Gas Light" (1938) and its film adaptation (1944), in which the main character manipulates his wife, causing her to doubt her memory and mental well-being. Since then, the word "gaslighting" has come to signify any attempt at manipulation aimed at making a person doubt their reality[301].

Signs of gaslighting include:

- Denying facts or events that actually happened.
- Distorting or substituting information.
- Undermining confidence in one's own perceptions and feelings.
- Conviction for doubts or questions.

---

[300] Book 2: Emotions and reason: keys to understanding relationships. The Brain as a Time Machine - Reality
[301] Manipulation

- Changing behaviors and moods without explanation.
- Ignoring or disregarding your concerns and feelings.

Consequences of gaslighting:

- Constant doubt in one's judgment and perception of reality.
- Feelings of isolation and loneliness.
- Anxiety, depression and increased irritability.
- Decreased self-esteem and self-confidence.
- Breakdown of trust in other people.
- Post-traumatic stress disorder (PTSD) in severe cases.

How to counter gaslighting:

- Social coping: Share your experiences with friends, family or professionals who can give you support and help[302].
- Trust your feelings and perceptions: Do not let the manipulator make you doubt yourself. Your perception of reality and your feelings matter.
- Write down facts and events: Keeping a record of your experiences and events can help you see a pattern of manipulation and verify your memories.
- Set boundaries: Define your boundaries and learn to say no to the manipulator. It is important to protect your space and your autonomy[303].
- Seek professional help: In some cases, you may need the help of a psychologist or therapist to resolve problems related to gaslighting.

Gaslighting is a dangerous form of psychological manipulation that can have serious consequences for the victim's mental health. Understanding the signs of gaslighting and teaching yourself how to resist it can help you protect yourself and your loved ones from manipulation and help you maintain your mental stability.

---

[302] Coping Strategies
[303] Book 11: The Science of Relationships: love, partnership, harmony in a couple. Boundaries

Gaslighting is often used by emotional abusers to blame the victim.

Victim Blaming

Victim blaming, is a psychological phenomenon in which the victim is blamed for the violence, discrimination or other abuse that has occurred.

Reasons for victim blaming:

- Maintaining the illusion of a just world: People tend to believe that the world is just and everyone gets what they deserve. This can lead them to look for the causes of the incident in the behavior of the victim rather than the actions of the abuser[304].

Belief in a just world or the phenomenon of a just world is a social-psychological phenomenon expressed in the belief that the world is organized justly and people in life get what they deserve according to their personal qualities and deeds: good people are rewarded and bad people are punished.

- Lack of information and understanding: People may be unfamiliar with the details of the incident or may not understand its implications, which can contribute to victim blaming[305].
- Stereotypes and prejudice: Societal stereotypes and prejudice can lead people to make assumptions about victims based on their gender, race, age or social status[306].

Consequences of victim blaming:

---

[304] Book 3: The Psychology of Relationships: Traumas, Defenses, Behavioral Styles. Cognitive Distortions, Locus of Control
[305] Book 5: How to find happiness: looking through the window of the world picture. Worldview, Attitudes, Developmental level
[306] Book 7: The logic of love: thinking in relationships. Misconceptions, Gender Stereotypes

- Reinforcing trauma: Blaming the victim can increase feelings of guilt, shame and stigmatization, which in turn exacerbates psychological trauma[307].
- Supporting Violence: Blaming the victim can reinforce a culture of violence by allowing abusers to avoid taking responsibility for their actions[308].
- Victim Silence: Victims may not talk about their experiences for fear of being blamed, which can lead to missed opportunities for support and justice[309].

A spiral of silence is a social psychological effect in which people tend to hide their opinions or not express them aloud if they feel that their point of view does not correspond to the generally accepted or dominant one in a certain social group.

For example, if a woman is a victim of sexual assault, she may be told that it was her own fault because she was dressed provocatively or was in the wrong place at the wrong time. If the victim does not feel supported by the community or friends, she may feel shame and humiliation, which may cause her to hide her experience and not talk about it[310].

This may lead others to be inclined to keep silent because they may feel that her experience is not up to a standard or norm and they do not want to cause annoyance or negative reactions from society. The spiral effect of silence can lead to a distorted view of what people really think.

Victim blaming is a serious problem faced by many victims of abuse and sexual assault. From the perspective of the abuser, the most

---

[307] Book 3: The Psychology of Relationships: Traumas, Defenses, Behavioral Styles. Personality disorders
[308] Marriage
[309] Book 10: Choosing the ideal partner. Masculinity and femininity. Femininity - Spiral of Silence
[310] Sexual Violence

common exculpatory argument heard in the courts is - implied consent.

Implied consent is consent that is not explicitly given by the person, but rather implicitly given by the person's actions and the facts and circumstances of a particular situation (the person's silence or inaction).

Therefore, in a relationship with a partner, it is important to clearly articulate one's consent or disagreement[311].

Sexual Violence

Rape culture is a social environment where rape is common and accepted because of societal attitudes about gender and sexuality[312].

Rape culture is a term describing a culture in which rape and sexual violence against women is commonplace and dominant attitudes, norms, practices and media normalize, tolerate or even condone sexual violence against women.

Examples of behaviors commonly associated with rape culture include victim blaming, sexual objectification, banalization of rape, denial of the prevalence of rape, and refusal to acknowledge the adverse consequences of sexual violence[313].

Sexual objectification is treating another person solely as a tool (object) for sexual gratification, without regard to the person's personality or ability to experience feelings.

---

[311] Book 10: Choosing the ideal partner. Masculinity and femininity. Femininity - The Principle of Consent, Communicating with a Partner
[312] Book 11: The Science of Relationships: love, partnership, harmony in a couple. Patriarchy
[313] Book 10: Choosing the ideal partner. Masculinity and femininity. Femininity - Sexual Objectification

Human objectification is the perception of a person as a commodity or object for some use. Human objectification is usually studied at the societal level, but it can also occur at the individual level[314].

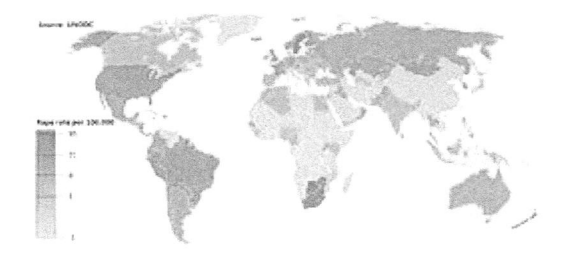

The map shows the prevalence of sexual violence around the world.

The reluctance to criminalize and prosecute non-consensual sex between spouses is due to traditional views of marriage, interpretations of religious doctrine, notions of male and female sexuality, and cultural expectations of the wife's subordination to her husband - views that are still prevalent in many parts of the world[315].

This continues to provoke protests from women demanding equal rights with men, as expressed in the basic thesis of Fimenism: my body is my business[316].

Public awareness of sexual violence perpetrated by women may be less prevalent or underestimated due to stereotypes about women's roles and ideas about sexuality. Sexual violence by women can include physical or verbal violence, sexual harassment, non-consensual sexual acts and other forms of sexual violence[317].

---

[314] Social Constructivism

[315] Book 11: The Science of Relationships: love, partnership, harmony in a couple. Patriarchy, Culture, Gender, State

[316] Book 10: Choosing the ideal partner. Masculinity and femininity. Gender Conflicts

[317] Types of sexual violence

Sexual violence: is any unwanted sexual act, attempted sexual act, or contact that occurs without the explicit or implied consent of one of the participants.

Some victims avoid categorizing the violence as sexual rape in order to reduce its significance and make it more tolerable. To do so, they use defense mechanisms to help them cope with the violence and continue to function in difficult circumstances.

Sexual violence is any type of unacceptable sexual behavior that occurs without consent, expressed clearly and voluntarily, and can include physical violence, threats, blackmail, use of force or threats of violence, as well as rape and other forms of sexual aggression[318].

The following types of sexual violence are distinguished:

- Rape: Forced sexual penetration of another person's body without their consent.

Generally, people only refer to this form of sexual violence, but there are other types of sexual violence besides direct rape.

- Non-consensual sexual activity: Sexual activities that occur without the clear and unambiguous consent of all participants. For example, when one party does not explicitly consent to sexual activity, but it occurs anyway[319].
- Voyeurism: The covert observation or filming of another person's intimate activities without their knowledge or consent. Voyeurs may use hidden cameras, wiretaps, or other means to observe people in private or intimate situations. This is illegal and unacceptable behavior that violates the privacy and boundaries of personal integrity of others. Voyeurism is a

---

[318] Book 10: Choosing the ideal partner. Masculinity and femininity. Femininity - The Consent Principle
[319] Book 10: Choosing the ideal partner. Masculinity and femininity. Femininity - Principle of Consent

form of sexual violence because it violates the right to privacy and creates a sense of vulnerability and fear in victims[320].
- Exhibitionism is the sexual pleasure of showing one's genitals or sexual acts to others without their consent. Exhibitionists usually seek excitement and gratification from the reaction or surprise of their victim. Exhibitionism can be considered a form of sexual abuse because it violates the sexual boundaries of others without their consent.
- Reproductive coercion is a form of violence or threat aimed at restricting a partner's reproductive rights and freedoms, as well as their health and decision-making in this area. This includes a set of tactics whose purpose is to coerce a partner into conceiving or terminating a pregnancy.
- Sexual Exploitation: Using a person's sexuality or intimacy for commercial or exploitative purposes without their free and informed consent. For example, using someone for the porn industry or forcing them to sell sexual services.
- Sexual abuse or ritual slavery: Humiliating, degrading, or causing physical or emotional harm by sexual acts.
- Child sexual exploitation (pedophilia): The use of children for the sexual gratification of adults, including sexual contact, pornography, or forced prostitution.
- Internet harassment: Violence and harassment committed over the Internet, such as sending obscene messages, making threats or distributing inappropriate material. As a subspecies, sexual privacy hacking.
- Sexual privacy hacking: is the unauthorized dissemination of sexual information or material, such as photos, videos or texts, without the consent of the owner. Example: when a person distributes intimate photos of their ex-partner without their consent.
- Use of pressure on sexual orientation: these are acts intended to control, manipulate or change another person's sexual

---

[320] Book 12: Motives for Marriage: Sex, Family, Parenting, Money. Sex - Sexual Attraction Disorders

orientation against their will. This may include pressure, threats, violence or discrimination.
- Coercion: The use of force, threats or manipulation to force another person to perform sexual acts against his/her will. For example, when a person threatens physical violence to obtain sexual consent.
- Stalking: is the repeated unwanted and persistent attention, stalking or observation of another person that causes the victim anxiety or fear. Example: when a person regularly follows the victim, shows up at the victim's workplace or home without consent.
- Harassment: is repeated unwanted, threatening, or persistent behavior that may cause anxiety, fear, or worry to the victim. Example: systematic insults or humiliation in the workplace.

Estimating the prevalence of spousal rape is difficult, especially outside the Western world. Discussing sexual matters is considered taboo in many cultures. One of the problems in researching spousal rape is that the Western concept of consent is not always understood or applied in many parts of the world.

Many cultures postulate social norms that **create a double standard of sexual morality:**

- one for sexual acts that occur within marriage and are viewed as an obligation that cannot be waived
- the other for non-marital relationships, which are considered wrong (or illegal/unacceptable).

The prevalence of marital rape varies according to the specific legal, national and cultural context. In 1999, the World Health Organization conducted a study on violence against women in Tajikistan. The survey was conducted among 900 women over the age of 14 in three districts of the country and found that 47% of married women had been forced to have sex by their husbands. In Turkey, 35.6% of women had been occasionally raped by their husbands and 16.3% had been raped frequently.

Regarding sexual violence of men by women, statistics show that about 13-16% of men are assaulted by their spouses or cohabitants during their lifetime.

Research by Morse, Strauss, and Gelles shows that men and women have about the same levels of victimization to violence by their partners or cohabitants[321].

Victimization is the process in which a person becomes a victim of crime, violence, or other harmful acts.

However, these data fall under the more general category of partner violence and do not reflect rates of spousal rape[322].

Unlike stranger rape or rape outside of marriage, where the victim may remove herself from the rapist and have no further contact with him, in the case of spousal rape, the victim is often left in a situation where there is no choice but to continue living together with her spouse. This is due to the difficulty of obtaining a divorce in many parts of the world and the stigmatization of divorce.

Divorce stigma is negative social attitudes and prejudice against people who choose divorce or are already divorced.

Researchers Finkelhor and Yullo noted in their study, "When a woman is raped by a stranger, she has to live with frightening memories. When she is raped by her husband, she has to live with her rapist."

Marriage, family, gender roles:

Women's gender roles contribute to the maintenance of violence. In many cultures, women believe it is their duty to sacrifice themselves for the family and fulfill their husbands' sexual needs for harmony and happiness. As a result, marital violence is normalized and women

---

[321] Book 9: Culture of love: norms, power, ethics. Culture of Silence
[322] Types of Sexual Violence

believe they are obligated to tolerate it. Violence becomes so embedded in society that women feel the need to adapt to it[323].

On the other hand, husbands face pressure on their masculinity and confront expectations associated with the roles of husband, father, and breadwinner. Men are expected to provide material well-being and protect the family. Along with these responsibilities come privileges and the authority of patriarchy. Thus, men may react to the threat to their power and authority from women, which can lead to violence[324].

Masculinity is associated with superiority and femininity with submission.

Researchers believe that violence may be men's way of reaffirming their masculine identity. Masculinity also involves restraining emotions, and the "masculine archetype" is the strong, resilient, and in control of one's emotions[325].

Some men may use violence to regain a sense of control. However, most men are not prone to violence. Ideals of masculinity may only play a role in violence for those who are prone to it. Research suggests a link between suppression of emotions and a tendency toward violence in some men. Suppression of emotions can lead to a buildup of negative emotions and stress, which can eventually translate into violent behavior[326].

Preventing sexual violence:

---

[323] Book 12: Motives for Marriage: Sex, Family, Parenting, Money. Marriage, Family
[324] Book 10: Choosing the ideal partner. Masculinity and femininity. Binary Gender System, Attitudes, Dysfunctional Patterns, Thinking Errors, Power
[325] Book 10: Choosing the ideal partner. Masculinity and femininity. Unconscious, Masculinity
[326] Book 2: Emotions and reason: keys to understanding relationships. Emotions

There are several approaches to preventing sexual violence:

- Prevention and education: Disseminating information about sexual violence, its consequences and how to protect oneself can help raise awareness and prevent such behavior. Educational programs in schools and community settings can teach people to recognize warning signs and provide them with the skills to behave safely and protect themselves.
- Social education: It is important to create a culture that does not tolerate sexual violence and recognizes the rights and dignity of every human being. Advocating for gender equality, respect and consent in relationships can help change negative perceptions and behaviors.
- Victim support: Developing and supporting accessible services for survivors of sexual violence, including confidential hotlines, crisis centers and professional assistance, helps survivors seek help and support. It is important to create safe spaces where victims can talk about their experiences and get the help they need.
- Ending impunity: Building a justice system that effectively investigates and addresses sexual violence sends the message that such crimes will not go unpunished. Punishing perpetrators and protecting the rights of victims play an important role in preventing sexual violence.
- Intervening in cultural norms: Changing cultural norms that promote or condone sexual violence is an important aspect of preventing such behavior. This includes challenging gender stereotypes, sexual discrimination and industrial exploitation.

Combining these approaches can help to better prevent sexual violence and create a safe environment for all people.

Economic violence:

Economic violence is a form of violence in which one party uses its economic power and control to oppress, manipulate or suppress another party[327].

Economic violence can have serious consequences for victims, limiting their freedom of choice, independence and ability to provide for themselves and their dependents. It can lead to financial dependency, poverty, social isolation and other negative consequences for the victim[328].

Economic or financial abuse is a form of violence in which one partner in a relationship controls the other's access to economic resources by using family assets for control.

The main difference between economic abuse and financial abuse is that economic abuse involves controlling a person's ability to earn money in the present and future by preventing them from obtaining employment or education.

Types of economic violence:

- Economic violence: is a form of domination and control that manifests itself by restricting the economic freedom and opportunities of another individual or group in order to subjugate and control their actions, ensure dependency or infringe on their rights. Example: One spouse threatens the other with financial deprivation if he or she decides to break off the relationship, resulting in the restriction of the victim's freedom of choice and subjugation.
- Material abuse or financial control: this is when one individual or group controls access to the financial resources of another individual or group by abusing their position and uses this as a means of pressure, manipulation or infringement. Example: A spouse controls the family budget, does not allow his wife

---

[327] Control, Boundaries, Human Rights, Manipulation, Object Relations Theory
[328] Book 11: The Science of Relationships: love, partnership, harmony in a couple. Co-dependency

- access to funds, demands an accounting of every item purchased, and threatens to cut household funds if she does not comply with his demands.
- Economic disadvantage: is the systematic imposition of economic obstacles, reduced access to resources or opportunities, resulting in inequality, discrimination or dependency for an individual or group, leading to the devaluation of their vital interests. Example: An employer fires or reduces an employee's salary because of the employee's race, sex, age, or other characteristics, resulting in devaluing the employee's professional opportunities and limiting his or her economic freedom.

Economic violence makes the victim dependent on the abuser, which can lead to restricted access to education, employment, career advancement and assets.

Being forced to sign documents, sell property, or change a will is also a form of economic abuse.

Some abusers may install apps to control the victim's spending and prevent them from spending without their consent, which can lead to the accumulation of debt or depletion of the victim's savings.

Disagreements over spending can also lead to additional violence in the form of physical, sexual or emotional abuse. In areas where women depend on their husbands' income, economic violence can have serious consequences, including maternal and child malnutrition[329].

For this reason, I recommended the partnership model of relationships, which on the one hand is more complex and requires a high level of development for both partners, but on the other hand, it is where the true understanding of love and harmony in a couple is revealed[330].

---

[329] Book 11: The Science of Relationships: love, partnership, harmony in a couple. Patriarchy - The breadwinner model, Culture of Silence
[330] Book 12: Motives for Marriage: Sex, Family, Parenting, Money. Partnership,

Consequences of domestic violence

Domestic violence has serious and long-lasting consequences for the victim:

- Physical injuries: The victim may experience various forms of physical violence, including bruises, fractures, abrasions, scrapes, grazes, burns and other types of injuries. This can lead to health problems, chronic pain syndromes, restricted movement, and physical disabilities.
- Psychological problems: Domestic violence can have a serious impact on a victim's mental health. The victim may experience persistent fear, anxiety, depression, post-traumatic stress disorder (PTSD), decreased self-esteem, feelings of guilt, insomnia, and other psychological problems.
- Social isolation: Victims of domestic violence may feel isolated from their family, friends, and community. The abuser may increase control over the victim by limiting contact with the outside world, which can lead to social isolation and loss of support.
- Relationship Problems: Domestic violence can negatively affect the victim's relationships with family, friends and partners. The victim may have difficulty establishing healthy boundaries, trust and emotional intimacy in future relationships.
- Economic hardship: The abuser may control the victim's finances by limiting the victim's access to financial resources or forcing the victim to remain in a violent situation. This can lead to economic hardship, financial dependency, and loss of financial independence.

Impact on children:

If there is domestic violence in the family, children may also witness or be exposed to violence. This has a serious impact on their emotional and psychological well-being. Children who witness domestic violence may experience anxiety, fear, depression, have behavioral and developmental problems, and repeat violent patterns in their future relationships[331].

Violence destroys partnerships.

Violence in partnerships can lead to a serious breakdown of interpersonal bonds and fundamental aspects of partnerships.

Here's how violence can affect these aspects:

- Respect: Violence undermines respect between partners because the abuser shows disregard for the victim's physical and emotional well-being.
- Trust: Violence destroys trust between partners by creating fear, insecurity and apprehension about each other's safety and reliability.
- Dignity: Violence can damage a victim's self-esteem and diminish their sense of self-worth, making it difficult to establish and maintain healthy relationships, withstand boundaries, and be independent.
- Honor: Violence destroys honor, leading to partners who may feel betrayed, humiliated, and not valued. Which in turn destroys loyalty.
- Accountability: The abuser often does not accept responsibility for his or her actions, shifting blame to the victim, which destroys trust and fairness in the relationship.
- Self-reliance: Abuse victims may lose the ability to rely on themselves and make decisions as the abuser attempts to control and dominate them.

---

[331] Book 12: Motives for Marriage: Sex, Family, Parenting, Money. Children

- Honesty: The abuser may use lies and manipulation to control the victim, which destroys the principles of honesty and candor in the relationship.
- Sincerity: Violence can lead to a loss of sincerity in a relationship because partners may hide their feelings, fears and concerns to avoid additional violence or conflict.
- Openness: In abusive relationships, openness between partners may decrease. Victims may be afraid to express their thoughts and feelings for fear of the abuser's reaction. This can lead to misunderstandings and emotional alienation between partners.

The effects of these destructive behaviors can be seen throughout life, affecting the ability to participate in healthy relationships and overcome trauma.

However, with support, professional help and therapy, it is possible to restore these values and build happy, healthy relationships in the future[332].

Why interest is lost

A key factor in the loss of interest is the different level of development of the partners, as a result of which they no longer understand each other[333].

In general, there are many reasons why a woman may lose interest in a man or vice versa. It is important to note that the reasons can be conscious or unconscious, intrapersonal or interpersonal, fixable or unfixable, as I have described throughout the book[334].

Here are some common factors that can lead to loss of interest:

---

[332] Book 12: Motives for Marriage: Sex, Family, Parenting, Money. Family Therapy
[333] Book 6: Developmental level. Maturity of the partner. Spiral Dynamics, Crises
[334] Book 6: Developmental level. Maturity of the partner. Conflicts

- Loss of love: Is one of the most common factors and is primarily related to a crisis that occurs when a couple moves to another level of integration[335].
- Lack of attraction: Physical or intellectual attraction may fade over time, especially if the couple does not put effort into maintaining this aspect of the relationship.
- Addiction: When a relationship becomes too predictable, boredom occurs. The desire for new experiences and change may prompt a woman to seek interest outside of the current relationship[336].
- Lack of emotional intimacy: If a man and a woman cannot establish a deep emotional connection, the woman may lose interest in the relationship.
- Communication problems: A lack of openness, honesty, or empathy in communication can lead to frustration and alienation[337].
- Incompatible values and life priorities: Over time, it may become clear that the man and woman have different outlooks on life, making it difficult for the relationship to grow[338].
- Lack of support: If partners do not support each other in personal or professional situations, this can lead to a loss of interest.
- Changing Life Circumstances: Life changes, such as family commitments or moving, can lead to misalignment and loss of interest.
- Sexual Problems: If a couple's sex life becomes monotonous or unsatisfying, it can reduce the man's attractiveness in the eyes of the woman.

---

[335] Book 12: Motives for Marriage: Sex, Family, Parenting, Money. Loss of love, Stages of relationship development, Family crises
[336] Book 1: The biology of relationships: why people form couples. Cheating
[337] Book 11: The Science of Relationships: love, partnership, harmony in a couple. Communicating with a Partner, Communication
[338] Book 6: Developmental level. Maturity of the partner. Spiral Dynamics, Values, Worldviews

- External influences: Friends, family, or coworkers may put pressure on a woman to reevaluate her relationship and lose interest in her partner[339].
- Unresolved conflicts: If there are unresolved issues or conflicts in a man-woman relationship that are not discussed or ignored, this can lead to a loss of interest.
- Toxicity and Destructive Behavior: A woman may lose interest in a man if he exhibits toxic, manipulative, or aggressive behavior[340].
- Violence: Is a major factor in destroying relationship[341].
- Self-development and changing interests: In the process of individual growth and self-development, the interests and preferences of partners can change, which can lead to a loss of interest.

Loss of interest in a partner can be the result of many factors and does not always indicate relationship problems or partner deficiencies. In some situations, people lose interest in a partner due to internal biopsychosocial reasons[342].

What destroys relationships:

Relationship breakdown can be caused by many factors and usually each unhappy family experiences its own problems and difficulties, which disproves the stereotype that "all families are unhappy in the same way, but happy in their own way".

The feeling of happiness or unhappiness is related to the developmental level of the couple.

At each level, the emphasis is different[343].

---

[339] Book 13: Communicating with your partner. Manipulation. Conflict Management. Communicating with a Partner, Communication
[340] Toxicity, Passive Aggression, Manipulation, Abuse
[341] Violence
[342] Book 1: The biology of relationships: why people form couples. Love, Biopsychosocial Structure of Personality, Mistakes in Partner Selection
[343] Book 11: The Science of Relationships: love, partnership, harmony in a

I've described the main motives and reasons in the chapter on divorce[344].

I'll highlight the common reasons that can cause a relationship to break up:

- Psychological factors: inadequate behavior, distorted perceptions and reactions can cause conflicts and frustration between partners.
- Differences in outlook: differences in values, upbringing and ideas about life can lead to misunderstanding and irritation.
- Environmental influences: the opinions of friends, relatives and society can affect the partner's evaluation and behavior, which can cause divergent views and conflicts.
- Incompatibility on an instinctive level: sometimes partners are simply not suited to each other in terms of character, temperament or biochemistry, which can lead to antipathy and dislike.
- Differences in spirituality: disagreement in meanings and values related to spiritual matters can cause disagreement and conflict between partners.

The key to a happy family is the right choice of partner, awareness, responsibility, adequacy, congruence, autonomy and a high level of development of both partners[345].

The Four Horsemen of the Apocalypse:

John Gottman, a well-known American psychologist and researcher of family relationships, identified several factors that destroy romantic

---

couple. Types of Relationships - Happy and Unhappy Relationships, Level of Couple Development

[344] Book 11: The Science of Relationships: love, partnership, harmony in a couple. Divorce

[345] Book 11: The Science of Relationships: love, partnership, harmony in a couple. Boundaries, World Picture, Mental Health, Expectations from Partner, Developmental Level section

relationships. He called them the Four Horsemen of the Apocalypse, similar to the biblical view of the end of the world.

These four factors can lead to relationship breakdown if they are not addressed or controlled:

- Criticism: Constant criticism of the partner can lead to resentment and negative emotions. Gottman suggests replacing criticism with complaints expressed in a more constructive and sensitive way[346].
- Demonstrating contempt: Openly expressing contempt, ridicule, or sarcasm can cause feelings of resentment and severely damage the relationship. Instead, Gottman recommends showing respect for your partner and focusing on their positive qualities[347].
- - Defensive Reaction: When one partner becomes defensive and responds to accusations, it can cause additional conflict and misunderstandings. Gottman suggests taking responsibility for one's actions and apologizing if necessary[348].
- Avoiding conflict: Avoiding conflict and refusing to discuss problems can lead to a buildup of negative emotions and frustration. Gottman recommends openly discussing problems and seeking resolution, as well as maintaining an emotional connection with your partner[349].

In addition to these four factors, Gottman also explored other aspects that can influence the success of a romantic relationship, such as emotional intelligence, communication skills, and the ability to show love and care. Working through these aspects can help a couple cope and strengthen their relationship.

---

[346] Passive Aggression, Communicating with your partner

[347] Toxicity, Psychological Abuse

[348] Defense Mechanisms, Coping, Assertiveness

[349] Book 13: Communicating with your partner. Manipulation. Conflict Management. Conflict Management, Emotional Intelligence

What we're together for?

So, above we have considered various aspects of personal and interpersonal understanding of the essence of romantic relationships and marriage. Of course, not all aspects have been listed and taken into account, as each person's life is filled with an individual understanding of happiness and harmony[350].

For some people, harmony in relationships may mean mutual understanding, support, and the ability to share each other's joys and difficulties. For others, harmony may manifest itself in shared achievement of goals, mutual support in professional growth or personal development. For some people, it is important to have common interests and hobbies that help them spend time together and enjoy each other's presence. It is worth noting that each couple has their own unique ideas about harmony and happiness.

What may be important to some may not be so important to others.

Therefore, understanding what brings true happiness and harmony in a relationship is an individual process that requires open communication, mutual respect and compromise. Ultimately, the foundation of a healthy and happy relationship is mutual love, respect and understanding between partners.

People enter into relationships and marriage for a variety of reasons.

In terms of motives, we can talk about the satisfaction of needs. For some it is legal sex, a source of livelihood or a way to gain higher social status and importance. For others it is sensual priorities - love and harmony. For others, the motives are focused on having children and conforming to general ideas of happiness[351].

---

[350] Book 11: The Science of Relationships: love, partnership, harmony in a couple. Marriage, Couple Harmony, World Values Survey, Thinking, Personality, World View

[351] Book 5: How to find happiness: looking through the window of the world picture. Happiness, Needs

In this description, needs and values, i.e., motives and goals, are mixed. Most people do not have such a clear differentiation, as it requires complex analysis and requires a lot of time and effort[352].

In terms of needs, the following reasons for entering into a relationship can be mentioned.

- Need for love and acceptance: People seek a partner who will love, appreciate and accept them for who they are. This is related to the desire for emotional support and intimacy.
- Need for security: Marriage and romantic relationships can provide a sense of security and stability. Partnerships can provide support and protection in difficult situations as well as reinforce a sense of belonging.
- Need for sexual intimacy: Physical attraction and intimacy are important aspects of romantic relationships and marriage. People seek a partner with whom they can share and fulfill their sexual needs.
- Need for a partner to grow together: People seek a partner with whom they can grow and develop together. This may include career development, personal growth, education, or building a future together.
- Need for a companion or friend: Marriage and romantic relationships provide an opportunity to share life with another person, including daily joys and challenges, starting a family, raising children, and building a future together.
- Need for social belonging: Relationships and marriage can fulfill the need for belonging and social support. With a partner, people can feel part of a wide circle of family, friends, and community.
- Need for emotional support and understanding: Romantic relationships and marriage provide opportunities to receive emotional support, understanding and empathy from a

---

[352] Book 6: Developmental level. Maturity of the partner. Level of Development, Thinking

partner. A sense of closeness and trust allows people to open up to each other and share their emotions and experiences.
- The need for a partner for mutual growth: People seek a partner who will inspire, motivate and help them become better versions of themselves. The shared pursuit of goals and support for self-development are important aspects of romantic relationships.
- The need for a partner to share joy and happiness: Marriage and romantic relationships allow people to share joyful moments, have fun together, and create happy memories. This can include different types of entertainment, traveling, and simply enjoying each other's presence.
- The need to start a family and continue the family: For some people, marriage and romantic relationships are linked to the desire to start a family, have children and continue the family lineage. Establishing a strong and stable family unit may be an important goal in their lives.

At the heart of these reasons are the needs for love, acceptance, support, intimacy, and growth, which romantic relationships and marriage can help fulfill.

Let me remind you about values, or rather their division into values of ends and values of means, because the above needs are revealed in values in other ways.

Depending on your individual and couple value structure, the surrounding reality and the meaning of the couple relationship are filled with different content[353].

What happy families have in common
There are several factors that bring happy couples together in the context of a romantic relationship or family:

---

[353] Book 6: Developmental level. Maturity of the partner. Spiral Dynamics, Level of Couple Development

- Mutual trust: Happy couples know how to trust each other and feel that their partners rely on them.
- Respect: Happy couples respect and appreciate each other, recognizing and accepting their differences and individuality.
- Communication: Open and honest communication is the key to a happy relationship. It helps the couple to understand each other better and solve problems that arise.
- Mutual support: They support each other in difficult times and rejoice in their partner's successes.
- Shared values and interests: Shared hobbies and similar outlooks on life strengthen the bond between partners.
- Sense of humor: Being able to laugh together and enjoy life is an important aspect of a happy relationship.
- Compromise: Happy couples are able to compromise and find solutions that suit both partners.
- Financial Stability: While money is not a major factor in the happiness of a relationship, financial stability and a consistent view of money can help avoid conflict.
- Physical closeness and intimacy: Love and affection are stronger when couples regularly express their love through physical closeness and intimacy.
- Time spent together: Happy couples value the time they spend together and make an effort to pay attention to each other.

These factors, although they may vary depending on the individual characteristics of the couple, are common to many happy relationships and families.

Summarizing information about happy couples, the following factors can be identified:

- Diversity of sources of happiness: happy couples find happiness at different stages of life and in different circumstances.
- Communication: sharing experiences and knowledge helps happy couples overcome problems.

- Autonomy: partners are able to fulfill their needs and desires independently.
- Attention to each other's feelings and needs: happy couples strive to meet their partners' needs.
- Retention of individual interests and hobbies: couples do not lose their interests and hobbies while maintaining their "self".
- Interchangeability: partners complement each other and can replace each other in some situations.
- Separation: respecting and preserving the independence of the partners' views and opinions.
- Traditions: joint observance of traditions strengthens the relationship.
- Common outlook: similar values, life goals and perspectives.
- Financial compatibility: similar level of income and social status.
- Common food preferences: similar taste preferences.
- Agreement in upbringing and development of children: a common approach to the upbringing of children.
- Harmony in touch and physical intimacy: understanding each other's love languages.
- Ability to maintain stability in the relationship and inner state.
- Respect for the boundaries and interests of the partner.
- Harmonious sexual relationships: the importance of sexual compatibility.
- Caring for the psychological needs of the partner.
- Ability to cope with crises and difficulties.
- Acceptance of self and partner, as well as a realistic perception of oneself and one's desires.
- Common goal and shared interests: having joint plans and hobbies.
- Humor and play: the importance of lightness and fun in relationships.
- Protecting and supporting your partner: willingness to help and protect each other.
- Caring and accepting care: mutual care and support.

- Not fighting with your partner: accepting each other's shortcomings.
- Preserving and restoring the partner's self-esteem: being able to express their emotions and feelings.
- Relationship agreements: partners discuss and agree on their relationship.
- Compatibility in family roles: both partners have a similar pattern of separation from the family.
- Balance of comfort and sacrifice: ability to find compromises.
- Similar cultural and attitudinal level: common level of development and interests.
- Shared vision of the future and a common worldview: understanding of the couple's common goals and aspirations.
- Maturity: the ability to take responsibility and make intelligent decisions.
- Separation from previous relationships: the process of separating from previous relationships.
- Finding a new self-identity: the formation of a shared "We" in the relationship.
- Developing trust: openness and honesty in communication, willingness to trust each other.
- Emotional support: the ability to provide support and care in difficult moments.
- Adapting to change: the ability to adapt to new circumstances and situations.
- Conflict resolution: the ability to discuss problems and find compromises to resolve conflicts.
- Sharing responsibilities: equitable division of household and family responsibilities between partners.
- Showing tolerance: respecting the partner's opinion and feelings, tolerating his/her shortcomings.
- Openness to development: readiness for self-development and development of the relationship.
- Romance and intimacy: keeping romantic and intimate moments in the relationship.

- Loyalty: faithfulness and devotion to the partner.
- Joint decision-making: the ability to discuss and make decisions together.
- Non-manipulation: the desire for direct and honest communication without manipulation.
- Willingness to forgive: the ability to forgive mistakes and misunderstandings.
- Absence of addictions: independence from bad habits and co-dependencies.
- Mutual understanding and tolerance: the ability to listen to and understand each other, to respect differences in views and opinions.

Happy couples build their relationships on the basis of mutual understanding, trust, respect and support. They are able to overcome difficulties, grow together and make long-term plans. Such couples retain their individuality but also find shared interests and goals. An important aspect of a happy relationship is the ability to accept and love one's partner for who they are and to strive for their common well-being.

Conclusion

The book "Aggression, Toxicity, Violence, Abuse. What We're Together For?" provides the reader with a comprehensive exploration of the topic of aggressive and violent behavior in the context of family and romantic relationships. This work helps to understand and deal with the root causes and patterns of aggression, the relationship of aggression to personality characteristics, and the concept of toxicity.

The book also introduces the reader to the biopsychosocial underpinnings of violence and its relationship to developmental level. Special attention is given to aspects of violence such as physical, psychological, sexual, and economic violence.

Not only are the effects of violence explored, but also the causes of loss of interest in relationships. "The Four Horsemen of the

Apocalypse," representing negative communication patterns, explains how destructive factors, can undermine the stability of any relationship.

Ultimately, the reader will confront and find answers to the question, "What We're Together For?" by exploring what happy families and coping strategies have in common. Overall, this book will be a valuable resource for anyone seeking to understand and improve their family and romantic relationships.

In response to the questions posed at the beginning of the book, the following conclusions can be drawn:

- Aggression in humans arises from a variety of sources, including biological, psychological, and social factors. Men and women display aggression differently due to biological and sociocultural differences.
- Affection and aggression can be linked when unbalanced relationships, addictions, and unhealthy communication patterns are present.
- Passive aggression is a form of non-constructive expression of resentment or anger that is implicit. Its triggers can be stress, resentment, and fear of direct conflict.
- Coping with aggression involves managing emotions, developing assertiveness skills, and utilizing problem-solving strategies.
- A person's developmental level can affect their ability to manage aggression, which emphasizes the importance of personal and emotional development.
- Toxicity in relationships is often associated with aggression and violence. Avoiding toxic relationships is essential for health and well-being.
- Violence, including domestic and intimate violence, can have serious consequences for victims and witnesses.

- Harassment and victim-blaming can exacerbate the harms of psychological violence and they are often linked to power inequalities in relationships.
- Economic violence is the control of economic resources and can be used as a means of manipulation and control.
- Destructive relationships can escalate for many reasons including fear, dependency, and lack of alternatives.
- Building a happy relationship requires mutual respect, effective communication, honesty and balance.
- Partners who know how to create harmony in relationships usually have a talent for empathy, tolerance, and the ability to forgive.

Overall, the book emphasizes the importance of mindfulness, self-reflection, and relationship learning in overcoming aggression and violence.

Answers to many unaddressed questions, you can find in other books in the "Formula of Love" series:

- "Biology of Relationships: Why People Form Pairs."
- "Emotions and Reason: Keys to Understanding Relationships."
- "Psychology of Relationships: Trauma, Defenses, Behavior Style."
- "Need for Love. Value of Relationships."
- "How to Find Happiness: A Window into the World's View."
- "Level of Development. Partner Maturity."
- "The Logic of Love: Thinking in Relationships."
- "Harmony of Personality: Self-esteem in Relationships."
- "Culture of Love: Norms, Power, Ethics."
- "Choosing the Ideal Partner. Masculinity and Femininity."
- "The Science of Relationships: Love, Partnership, Harmony as a Couple."
- "Motives for Marriage: Sex, Family, Upbringing, Money."
- "Communication with a Partner. Manipulations. Managing Conflict."

- "Aggression, Toxicity, Violence, Abuse. Why Are We Together?"
- "Formula of Love."

Reading the entire series will allow you to find solutions to various problems that couples face.

A Note:

The purpose of the Formula of Love book series is to outline the general field of romantic relationships, identify important details, show cause and effect, and provide a handy toolkit for individual and couples work.

The course is based on a number of publicly available theories that explain and reveal the meaning of romantic relationships, love, affection, etc.

*A **theory** is an ordered and substantiated system of views, judgments, provisions, allowing to adequately explain facts, analyze processes, predict and regulate their development; a level of cognition at which knowledge about the subject of research is generalized and systematized and concepts, categories, judgments, inferences are formulated.*

Self-improvement. Disclosure of mechanisms and principles given in various theories is limitless. Therefore, my task is to show the model itself. Adaptation to your relationships, you will have to do on your own, because everything is individual. This is your personal growth and development as a path to happy and harmonious relationships.

Responsibility. In the course there is an author's position, not always coinciding with the generally accepted. Judgments and conclusions of the author should be taken as general educational and recommendatory. For each specific case, it is necessary to seek the help of a specialized specialist[354].

---

[354] Book 12: Motives for Marriage: Sex, Family, Parenting, Money. Psychological help, Family therapy

The examples are hyperbolized for educational purposes, to emphasize the contrast of the idea. Almost all examples are collective, i.e., they do not violate people's personal privacy.

The context of the situation changes the meaning. I tried to cut off irrelevant context as much as possible, as it is impossible to take into account all the diversity of life situations. Therefore, when reading the example, you may have associations from personal experience that do not match the conclusions. This is normal. Critically evaluate the material in the book and double-check the information.

I have used the word "partner" to refer to both women and men, both in romantic relationships, in the dating and partner selection stage, and in partnerships or marital relationships.

In the footnotes, I provide references to chapters that provide more detailed information related to the point being made. In the beginning I tried to avoid such hyperlinks so that you would not be distracted from the direction of the thought, but the further you go, the more often such links are indicated, as the material grows into a complementary context, presented in different chapters. If you remember the chapter in question and understand why the reference is given, you don't need to reread it. But if you don't understand why the chapter title is at the end of the sentence, then I recommend rereading it, again.

Repetition is the mother of skill. At the first reading a number of statements may not be perceived for various reasons: information may conflict with personal knowledge and beliefs, you may lack life experience, knowledge may be perceived for the first time, the level of development may not correspond to the material, cognitive distortions may be triggered, etc. However, upon re-reading, you will better understand the structure of the course and uncover a number of meanings that may have slipped through the cracks the first time you read it.

Ideas challenged by science. To simplify, structure, and/or explain complex phenomena, the course presents models that are outdated, challenged, or considered pseudoscientific. For example, Freud's structure of the psyche (Id, Ego, Superego), Paul McLean's model of the triple mind (snake, monkey, and human), Dilts' pyramid, and others. Also, I show character accentuations as a more convenient or familiar concept for typing people than the classification from the ICD-11.

Simplification of terms. In order not to delve into the biochemistry of the body and the workings of the nervous system, as this is not the goal of the course, although it does have an impact, I will not separate hormones (affect organ function), neurotransmitters (function in the brain and nervous system), and other signaling and regulatory molecules, but will use the word hormones. Similar simplifications may occur in other chapters.

Sometimes I will cite early theories and show their development. In this case, it is easier to show the starting point and convey the general concept of the development of the idea. For example, Hippocrates' temperament is the Functional Ensemble of Temperament (FET). Piaget's stages of cognitive development - Neopiagetian theories. Graves' theory of emergent cyclical levels of existence - Spiral Dynamics, and later Wilber's Integral Psychology and others. This development of the idea, removes questions about the internal logic of the theory.

The course can be complex and confusing. The point here is the general development of the human being. The ability to build connections between different blocks of information. Individual peculiarities of the brain and memory. If you do not understand any chapter, come back to read it later. Perhaps the material that follows will explain some details that will help you better understand the meaning of the chapter.

Communication between partners is the most important factor for the unity of a couple. This thesis, in various interpretations, is cited many times as one of the fundamental ones. What is important is the quality of communication revealed in the section "Communication".

Errors in the book. A number of my conclusions are subjective and this is natural, since I have personal life experience and individual beliefs. Also, there are errors in the logic of arguments reflected in different chapters. This is due to the computing power of my mind, as well as the lack of unambiguous understanding in modern science.

There may be errors in the names of authors, names of theories and statistical generalizations, which is due to the "hallucinations" of ChatGPT used in the work, so I apologize in advance to the authors if their surname is given incorrectly or not at all.

Copyright and Sources

Wikipedia is the primary source of information for the course. This is due to the objectivity, verifiability, accessibility and reliability of the information, as well as the ability to use quotations and images without violating copyright.

In some cases, I used materials of other authors, indicating their names or titles of works in the process of narration.

The text was created with the help of ChatGPT (https://chat.openai.com), which was used to collect, compare and analyze materials.

The cover art was created with a paid subscription from Midjourney (https://www.midjourney.com).

This book contains material taken from Wikipedia (https://wikipedia.org) of various countries including EN, RU, UA, FR, etc. between 2018 and 2023. All the material I used was freely available for use, according to Wikipedia's rules.

Made in the USA
Las Vegas, NV
10 April 2024

88518730R00095